BOWLING

D1560329

Sports Illustrated Winner's Circle Books

BOOKS ON TEAM SPORTS

Baseball
Basketball
Football: Winning Defense
Football: Winning Offense
Hockey
Lacrosse
Pitching
Soccer

BOOKS ON INDIVIDUAL SPORTS

Bowling
Competitive Swimming
Cross-Country Skiing
Figure Skating
Golf
Racquetball
Running for Women
Skiing
Tennis
Track: Championship Running
Track: Field Events

SPECIAL BOOKS

Backpacking
Canoeing
Fly Fishing
Scuba Diving
Small-Boat Sailing
Strength Training
Training with Weights

Sports Illustrated

BOWLING
Styling Your Game for Success

by Herm Weiskopf
and Chuck Pezzano

Photography by Heinz Kluetmeier

Sports Illustrated

Winner's Circle Books
New York

Special thanks to Dick Corley, Mike Corley, and Joe Stuart of Ethan Allen Lanes, Burlington, Vermont.

Library of Congress Cataloging in Publication Data
Pezzano, Chuck.
   Sports illustrated bowling.

   Reprint. Originally published: New York : Harper & Row, © 1981.
   1. Bowling.   I. Weiskopf, Herm, 1934- II. Kluetmeier, Heinz. III. Sports Illustrated (Time, inc.) IV. Title.
GV903.P45   1987   794.6   87-23510

Contents

"So what if my form's not perfect? At least I've got my eyes on the target, and with my style there's no worry about backswing, grip or slide. So here goes."

1

The Lure of the Game

Who bowls? Everybody. Well, almost everybody, or so it seems. Children too young to execute a full approach stand near the foul line and, using two hands, gleefully shove the ball down the line. Teen-agers, middle-agers, even octogenarians frequent the lanes. And there are countless leagues for bowlers of all types and abilities. Indeed, no other sport in the world has such a diversity of participants. Why? Bowling is fun; good, clean, laugh-it-up fun. It has become a big game, far bigger than most people are aware of.

Every hour of every day of every year, Americans bowl. Some bowling centers are open twenty-four hours a day, peopled during off-peak hours by "moonlight" leagues, nightshift workers and early risers. More than sixty million Americans bowl a staggering total of more than two billion games annually, figures that may be a bit hard to fathom. Easier to grasp are the results of surveys that have proved the same thing time after time: The No. 1 all-weather sport in the nation is bowling.

Part of the fun of the game is that it is very social. At the lanes, the atmosphere usually is homey, there are friends and neighbors to gab with, and everyone seems to have a good time.

1

The lanes are a nice place to see old friends, sit back and relax, take a look at other bowlers' scores and laugh and swap stories.

And bowling has become a sport that men and women can enjoy together, as well as a game that entire families can take part in. The game crosses all economic, age, cultural, ethnic and racial barriers. Indeed, bowling has become a very real part of almost every American's heritage, a part of growing up, a part of the good times to be remembered from the past, a part to be savored today and enjoyed again tomorrow.

Bowling is able to fill the needs of so many people because it is, above all, a simple game: The rules are not complex and the basics of how to roll the ball are quickly learned. Oh, the sport has considerable depth to it and there is no end to the complexities for those who really get into it, as a later chapter will reveal. But there has probably never been anyone who has not looked down a lane at those 10 pins and not thought, "Hey, this is easy. I can knock those down." With that in mind, just about everyone has given the game a try. And just about everyone has had the pleasure of toppling those pins.

Bowling is also one of those rare games that can be enjoyed as much by those who struggle to achieve middling scores as by those who consistently perform well. Newcomers soon find, too, that rolling a gutterball is nothing to be embarrassed about. Indeed, the off-target bowler is apt to guffaw as loudly about his miss as anyone else. Laughter, bowlers quickly discover, is as much a part of the sport as the pins and the balls.

As bowlers improve and try to master the game, many are captivated by the technicalities of the sport. For them, the enjoyment comes from trying to comprehend how and why pins and balls react the way they do under varying conditions. These bowlers constantly read and practice the latest theories concerning hand release, angles of delivery, ball rotation, and pin deflection. They experiment with newfangled gadgets and with variations of finger span and pitch. All this in the search for the perfect game.

LEAGUE BOWLING

League play is the hub around which bowling revolves, with more than ten million members participating on a regular basis. There are leagues for grade schoolers, high schoolers, collegians, senior citizens, classic leagues for high-average rollers, industrial leagues, church leagues, leagues for fraternal groups and for the handicapped, including the blind and those in wheelchairs.

Joining a league is easy and inexpensive. Advice about how to do so can be obtained at any bowling center. League seasons generally run from September to May, and the standings and averages are often posted on bulletin boards at the lanes. Each league has a president and treasurer, and every team has a captain. And all leagues are conducted according to strict rules set down by the sport's three main governing bodies—the American Bowling Congress, which is for men only, the Women's International Bowling Congress, and the American Junior Bowling Congress. The ABC, the WIBC, and the AJBC collectively bestow some two million awards upon bowlers each year, handing out honors for everything from high scores to the conversion of difficult splits.

Don't think you are not qualified to join a league because you are new to the game or because your scores are too low. There are leagues for everyone. The great equalizer is handicapping, just as in golf. Under this system, each bowler is given a handicap based on his average score, low scorers receiving higher handicaps than those who roll big numbers. These handicaps are added to a bowler's actual score and help to even up the competition. Many leagues and tournaments are handicap affairs, thus giving everyone a chance to be a winner. Events in which handicaps are not used are designated as "scratch" bowling.

In addition to league competition, there are in excess of ten thousand amateur tournaments each year, many at the county, regional and state levels. Most have modest prize funds. Annual national tournaments are also run by the three Congresses: these last from sixty to ninety days and offer competition in singles, doubles and five-player team categories, as well as an all-events category, which determines the winning total based on the scores achieved in the other three. There are separate divisions for low-scoring, high-scoring and professional bowlers, and for senior citizens. These are among the most massive sporting events in the world, each drawing some thirty thousand bowlers annually. The ABC offers a grand jackpot worth about $1 million, and the WIBC purse is close to $750,000.

Professional bowling has flourished in recent years, especially the Professional Bowlers Association, which is for men only. PBA tournaments are held almost weekly and all are now televised. Although the Women's Professional Bowlers Association has not yet attained comparable TV coverage, the growth is there.

Bowling has a somewhat unusual concept of distinguishing between professionals and amateurs. Only those bowlers who belong to the PBA or the WPBA are regarded as pros. All others are considered amateurs, even though some win more money than the professionals. This is possible because there are scads of nonprofessional tournaments that offer whopping payoffs.

Two of the most famous such tournaments are the Hoinke Classic in Cincinnati and the Petersen Classic in Chicago.

Starting in January of each year, the Hoinke is open for business seven days a week. When it is all over in October, fifty thousand amateur bowlers have shared in more than $1 million in prizes. Among the top awards are a new car for the man and the woman with the single game with the highest number of pins over their average; $30,000 to the victorious doubles team; $40,000 to the top-scoring team; and $50,000 to the singles champion.

While the Hoinke is a pretty straightforward tournament, the Petersen Classic, offering $700,000 in prizes, takes a very different approach to the game, making it the most distinctive bowling tournament anywhere.

Tournament director Mark Collor still conducts the Petersen in the same grubby place where it was first held in 1921. The Petersen is not sanctioned by the ABC or the WIBC, Collor deliberately making no effort to keep his lanes in tip-top shape. The home of the Petersen tournament is not well lighted or outfitted with comfortable settees, and is not equipped with the best of pins or the finest of lanes. Nevertheless, up to thirty thousand bowlers show up for the event year after year. This they do for two reasons: They are almost certain to be able to return home with some preposterous tales of what happened during the tournament; and they are well aware that they have as good a chance as anyone of earning a lucrative prize.

Collor's policy of neglect is calculated. His lanes are less than perfectly level or smooth, and unevenly oiled because he believes, and with good reason, that such lack of maintenance makes it hard for bowlers to come up with high scores. Those bowlers who do start off well must brace themselves to endure a multitude of distractions designed to harass them during later games. When a bowler is scoring well, he or she is sure to hear about it over a blaring public-address system at the lanes. Announcements, carefully calculated to distract, continue in an effort to rattle the bowler completely. Or a cat or a pigeon might suddenly appear on the lanes. Doors or windows are opened to allow blasts of frigid, wintry air to blow in. Maybe the last two games will have to be rolled on lanes so caked with oil that droplets of the stuff will fly off the ball as it rolls.

"Bowlers enjoy all this nonsense," Collor insists. "So we play it up. Our lane conditions are maintained conscientiously: The same for everybody— miserable. But equal. We do it to keep the scores down. We want to give duffers a chance to win something for a change. The last thing we want is for hotshot bowlers to come in here and earn all the money. This tournament is for the little guys." Indeed, bowling has many faces. And bowlers have lots of fun.

Bowling centers in the early days of the game were a far cry from those of today. Lanes were raised above the floor, balls clattered along wooden guide-rails as they were returned from the pits, and scores were kept on slates.

2

The Evolution of the Game

The earliest form of bowling dates back more than seven thousand years. In *The Making of Egypt,* published in 1939, Sir Flinders Petrie, professor of Egyptology at the University of London, wrote that he had found a complete set of bowling implements at a large gravesite where a child had been buried in about 5200 B.C. The items unearthed included several small stone balls, three oblong pieces of marble and nine slender stone pins. It was Petrie's belief that the three oblong pieces were used to form an archway through which the balls were rolled at the pins, most likely arranged in a diamond formation.

Bowling is sometimes referred to as "kegeling," a derivation from the next oldest-known form of the game practiced by the Germans as far back as the fourteenth century. Germans of that time carried a *Kegel,* a clublike weapon: Somehow the *Kegel* became a part of a unique church ritual in which people rolled round stones in the church cloisters, hoping to knock over the *Kegel,* believed to symbolize the *Heide,* or heathen. If a bowler struck down the *Kegel,* it was felt he had symbolically slain the heathen. Martin Luther (1483–1546) bowled at pins, although his objective was entertainment rather than part of any church rit-

8

FIRST YOU SET THEM UP, AND THEN—

Bowling scenes were often used by early political cartoonists, as can be seen from the front page of this 1886 newspaper (left) and from the manner in which Teddy Roosevelt was depicted in 1908 (right).

ual. Luther even had a bowling lane built for his children and reportedly "enjoyed their laughter when the ball went astray."

Abraham Lincoln was the first prominent American to frequent the lanes. It is not known, however, who the first person was to bowl in America, although it was the early German settlers who introduced the game into the American way of life, bowling often being a major part of their festivals and picnic gatherings. Chicago and New York were the first cities where the sport took root but, in those days, bowling was strictly an outdoor sport. Then, in the 1840s, the first indoor lanes were built in Manhattan, and soon the sport became a New York fad. In 1849 it was recorded that "on Broadway from Barclay Street to Eighth Street, there were alleys to be found on every block."

Varieties of bowling, most of it at ninepins, also flourished in New England during the 1800s, although many locales passed laws banning the sport, since it had a reputation of rowdyism and gambling. Somewhere along the line, a tenth pin was added, causing a rearrangement of the pins into an equilateral triangle, and various sets of rules for playing, scoring and equipment prevailed, leading to much confusion. It was not until the ABC was founded in Manhattan in 1895 that standards for all phases of the game began to take shape.

Although the ABC was (and is) for male bowlers only, women participated at private clubs and on church lanes. So, in 1916, the ladies banded together and formed a governing body of their own, one known today as the WIBC. Both the ABC and the WIBC now work together from headquarters in Greendale, Wisconsin, where they administer and enforce the rules of the game, certify lanes, and test all new equipment before it is approved for sanctioned competition. Both organizations also offer a full range of services covering every phase of the sport, including an extensive awards program. Sharing the office complex with the ABC and the WIBC is the American Junior Bowling Congress, which supervises most of the nation's youth programs. At the last count, the ABC had almost 5 million members, the WIBC 4.5 million and the AJBC close to 900,000. Among them, the three organizations sanctioned over 335,000 leagues.

Unlike many other sports, bowling has not had to make major alterations in the game to retain its popularity during the twentieth century. What has changed are the bowling centers. Years ago, many parents would not permit their children to go to bowling lanes because they were dark, dank and filled with seedy characters. No more. Today's bowling establishments are as well lighted, clean and wholesome as the most cautious parents could wish.

THE BOWLING CENTER TODAY

Modern bowling centers are designed to be homes away from home. In varying combinations, these establishments have lunch counters, restaurants, night clubs and bars. They also are equipped with nurseries and baby-sitters so the youngsters can rest or play while Mom and/or Dad rolls a few games. Some have carpeted walls to cut down on the noise from the clattering pins. An increasing number of centers have dazzling decors: chandeliers, water fountains or motifs ranging from Western to Colonial to ultramodern. At each center, the control desk is the hub of activity. It is there that lanes are assigned to bowlers, free scoresheets are passed out and bowling shoes are rented.

In the early days of bowling, many lanes were dank, poorly lit places crammed into basements filled with pillars and pipes. Note that the actual lane surface was raised and very narrow, making it almost impossible to convert many spares.

Around the turn of the century, lanes began to resemble those we know today. Here is a four-lane installation with full-width lanes, gutters and gravity ball-return tracks.

The advent of large, multilane centers such as this, with well-kept lanes, good lighting and convenient scoring, helped attract people to the game and enabled the sport to gain respectability.

Today's center offers the bowler all manner of luxury. Electronic scoring, comfortable seating, modern decor—just about everything to make your game more enjoyable.

The Lane

A bowling lane is an expensive "structure" built to demanding specifications. It stretches 62 feet, 10 $\frac{3}{16}$ inches from foul line to pit and measures exactly 60 feet from the foul line to the center of the No. 1 or head pin. A lane is between 41 and 42 inches wide, with the lane plus the two flanking gutters ranging from 60 to 60¼ inches. The surface must be free of continuous grooves and the tolerance for levelness is a mere 40/1,000 inch.

The approach (the area behind the foul line where the bowler starts) and the first 16-foot section of the lane are constructed of rock maple, a sturdy hardwood selected for its ability to resist the wear and tear of bowlers' feet and the constant impact of bowling balls. The middle of the lane, from the impact area to the pin deck, is constructed of pine, a softer wood, since it doesn't need as much durability because the ball is rolling by the time it passes the targeting arrows. However, hard wood is again used in the pin deck area. All the lane surface, maple or pine, is set in place tongue-and-groove fashion, using specially cut strips of wood appropriately called boards. Approximately 1-inch wide, each board is placed on edge and nailed, making a lane from 39 to 41 boards wide. In 1976 the first nonwood lanes were approved for use by the ABC, and since then several synthetic surfaces have come into use. No matter what a lane is made of, it is periodically inspected by the ABC before certification is issued to a proprietor.

As for those ten penguin-shaped pins, they are 15 inches tall, 4¾ inches around the thickest part of the belly and rest on a base that has a diameter of 2¼ inches. Approved pins weigh not less than 3 pounds, 2 ounces and not more than 3 pounds, 10 ounces. There cannot be a variance of more than 4 ounces between the heaviest and the lightest pins in any set. Years ago, pins were all wood. Now almost all are made of laminated hard maple, fitted with a plastic base and coated with plastic to increase their lifespan.

THE IMPACT OF AUTOMATION

Until 1952, pins were always set in place by pinboys who waited at the far end of the lanes to reposition them and return the balls to the bowler. In that year, the introduction of the first successful mechanized pinsetters marked the beginning of the end for pinboys and the start of a new era of bowling automation, and the most significant change in modern bowling. With proprietors no longer dependent upon pinboys, who were often in short supply, the game was speeded up and dressed up, and bowling centers rapidly expanded into huge complexes to accommodate the swift rise in the number of bowlers.

In the days before automatic pinsetters, pin-boys placed the pins on the lanes by hand. The semi-automatic setter, pictured above, enabled them to place the pins in slots in machines, which then lowered the pins to the deck. Development of the fully automatic pinsetter, a marvel of mechanical ingenuity (below), is largely responsible for the dramatic growth of the game.

Bowling is rapidly moving into the electronic age. Many centers now offer push-button automatic scorers (above) backed by highly sophisticated control desks (below), which allow the management to monitor lane activity closely.

Not long after automatic pinsetters came automatic scoring devices and score-projection units, which enabled bowlers to see their scores flashed above the playing area. Centers now even have automatic foul-detecting devices that utilize light beams to tell if a bowler's foot goes over the foul line. Bowling balls, which used to clatter back to the bowler on wooden racks that ran above the gutters, now whoosh back almost silently through under-the-floor channels. At the ball rack, bowlers now have the luxury of hand driers to dry their hands and get a sure grip on the ball.

To help you select a ball that is just the right weight, the pro will weigh it on a delicately balanced scale.

Equipment

One of the beauties of bowling is its simplicity. A good ball, a pair of bowling shoes, access to some lanes, and you're ready to roll. But, as in most sports, good equipment, properly selected and fitted, can make the difference between mediocre performance and a truly satisfying game. So take some time getting outfitted.

SELECTING THE RIGHT BALL

Weight

When selecting a ball, three things are important: weight, span and pitch. Bowling balls vary in weight from less than 10 pounds to a maximum of 16. Comfort and ease of handling are the main determinants in choosing a ball. It is usually safe to use the heaviest ball you can handle *without strain.* Beware of going with too heavy a ball. It will simply wear you down because each movement with a heavy ball—lifting it off the rack, holding it on the approach, positioning it for the pushaway and then taking it through the backswing and forward thrust—will take its toll. Most painful will be the aches and strains that will be

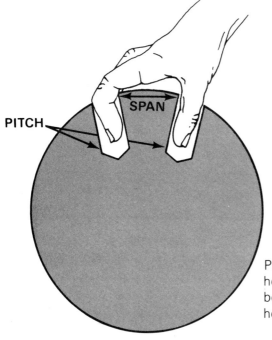

PITCH

SPAN

Pitch is the angle at which the finger holes are drilled. Span is the distance between the thumb hole and the finger holes.

there the next day. A ball may seem heavy until you swing it a few times, so take in a few practice swings with balls of different weights to get an idea of the weight that is best for you. On house balls provided free of charge by bowling centers, the weight is often stamped near the finger holes.

Men and boys, perhaps thinking that swinging a sixteen-pound ball will intimidate the pins or that it is the *macho* thing to do, are apt to start out using a ball that is too heavy. Remember that there is no other game in which the competitor makes so many throws with any object as hefty as a bowling ball. The goal is to wear down the pins, not the bowler. And keep in mind that a sixteen-pound ball will never do its job if the bowler is too tired to roll it properly.

For a conventional grip (A), the ball will fit properly when, with the thumb fully inserted into its hole, the second joints of the fingers stretch slightly over the inner edges of the finger holes (B).

A

B

Span and Pitch

Once you determine your proper ball weight, span is your next consideration. Span is the distance from the inner edge of the thumb hole to the inner edge of each of the finger holes. Find a ball with a thumb hole that allows the thumb to be inserted all the way to its base. The thumb should be loose enough to rotate, but not so loose that there is no friction or contact. Then, with the thumb in position, stretch your middle fingers over the finger holes—*over,* not into them. The crease of the second joints should extend about a quarter inch beyond the thumb side of the finger holes. The correct span allows fingers to be inserted just to the creases, so that a pencil will fit comfortably between your palm and the ball.

Pitch is simply the angle at which holes are drilled in the balls. Improper pitch can cause you to release the ball too soon or too late and can give you a feeling of not being comfortable with your ball. The amount of pitch needed will depend upon the length and flexibility of your fingers, and upon the type of grip used. To be certain you get the right pitch, go to the nearest pro shop. There you will be able to insert your fingers in a dummy ball that has a variety of finger holes and thumb holes. Precise measurements and hole drilling will then provide you with a fit that will be glovelike.

CUSTOM EQUIPMENT

Sooner or later, anyone seriously interested in bowling will want to buy fitted equipment. Where do you go for custom gear? Your local bowling center is a good place to start. The resident pro there can help you select the right ball and will drill it to fit your hand. But before being fitted, have the pro watch you bowl a few frames so he will get a feel for your style and know how you roll the ball. This will help him determine your exact specifications.

The right grip will be one of your considerations. For most people, the three-holed "conventional" grip is best. It is the easiest to control and the one used by most beginners. Only when your hand and arm have become stronger and when you have become a more proficient bowler should you try the other types of grips, the semi-fingertip grip and the full-fingertip grip. In the semi-fingertip, the holes are drilled so you can insert your fingers halfway up to the second joints. The full-fingertip grip requires even more strength because the holes are drilled only deep enough for the first joints.

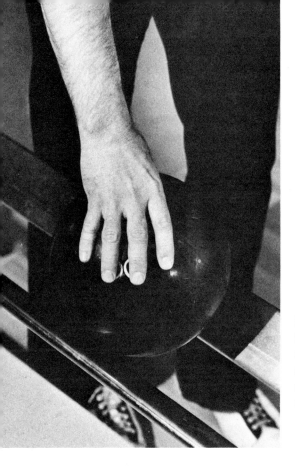

For the full fingertip grip, the crease of the first joints should fit just beyond the inside edges of the holes (left). Only the fingertips are inserted (right), which usually provides a more delicate control of the ball. This grip should be used only by experienced bowlers.

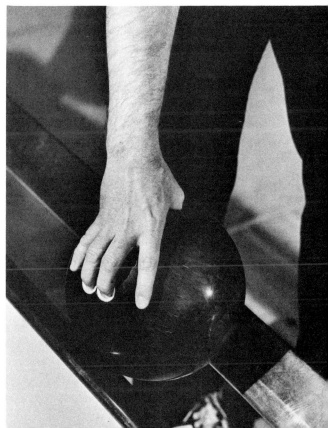

A   B   C

How important can a fitted ball be? WIBC Hall of Famer Doris Coburn insists, "The most important part of my game is a tight thumb hole. Once I discovered this years ago, my game improved considerably because a tight thumb hole is the key to a good armswing. You don't have to worry about holding onto the ball. The ball practically holds onto you. If I don't have to use my muscles to hold onto the ball, the armswing becomes very relaxed and gravity will cause the ball to swing like a pendulum."

Shoes

Aside from a ball, the only equipment a bowler *must* have is a pair of bowling shoes. Bowlers often talk about "right-handed shoes" and "left-handed shoes," which makes it sound like they wear them on their hands. Obviously, they don't. The nomenclature, however, is not really faulty, for the type of shoes a bowler wears depends on which hand a bowler rolls with. Each pair of shoes is designed to allow sliding and braking, one shoe for each purpose. For a right-handed bowler, the left shoe is soled with leather or similar material that

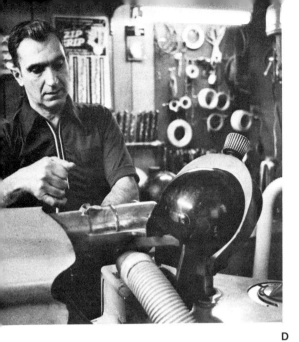

When custom fitting a ball, the pro will measure your thumb (A), fingers (B), and span (C), taking into account the type of grip you prefer. He then will drill the ball to your precise specifications using a special machine (D).

D

Bowling shoes are specially designed to serve vital functions. This pair, for a right-handed bowler, has an all-leather sole on the left shoe to permit an easy slide to the line, while the front of the right sole has an added piece of high-friction material to act as a brake for the right foot.

will permit him to slide easily to the finish of his delivery on that foot. Since the task of the right foot during the approach and at the finish is to provide traction and braking, the right shoe has a sole made of rubber or another high-friction material. Some rental shoes have identical soles that neither slide well nor brake well, so if you use them, make certain you know how they will affect your game while wearing them. And whatever shoes you wear, look out for grit so easily picked up on the soles. A quick brushing off (bowlers often use a small wire brush to do this) when necessary will prevent mishaps.

Clothing

Almost any type of clothing is acceptable in a bowling center: The prime consideration is comfort. Because bowling involves a lot of movement, loose-fitting apparel is best—as long as it does not interfere with the motion of the arms and the legs. So dress as you please. Just keep it loose.

Accessories

There are all sorts of accessories to help bowlers. Among the most popular are grip inserts for the finger holes, wrist straps, leg bands, gloves, weights, medications and material to help grip the ball more firmly or release it more easily. Before investing in such gimmicks, however, get advice about how they work and if they are likely to be of any value.

Of the above, the wrist strap is most commonly used because bowlers often find that a snug-fitting strap does what no amount of practice is able to accomplish: It locks their wrist in place. In addition to firming up the wrist, the strap enables you to forget about wrist positioning and, although it is no guarantee that the wrist will be in perfect alignment, it is generally effective. A strap may take some adjusting and getting used to, but it is usually worth its nominal cost.

Five items that many bowlers keep in their bowling bags are a hand towel, baby powder, a small cleaning cloth, rubbing alcohol and tape. The hand towel is to wipe the perspiration from your hands and face during a game. A sprinkling of baby powder will further dry the hands and prevent your fingers from becoming hung up in the ball. Use the rubbing alcohol on the cleaning cloth to wipe off the lane oil that accumulates on your ball as a game progresses. And the tape (plastic or electrician's tape are the best) can be placed in layers inside

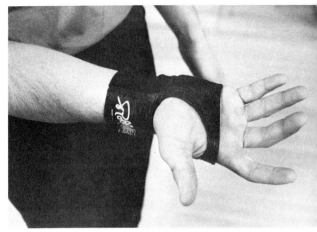

For many bowlers, a wrist strap is very helpful in keeping a firm wrist. Adjust the strap so that it fits snugly but allows you to move your hand and fingers comfortably.

the holes of the ball so the fingers will come out with less friction. Most people's fingers swell up a bit in humid weather or when rolling more than a few games. When this happens, bowlers who have taped finger holes are able to remove a layer or two of the tape at a time to provide whatever room is needed for their fingers. Any stickiness left from the tape can be removed from the hole by using a cloth soaked in rubbing alcohol or soapy water.

4

Getting Started

Many people of little athletic ability are far better bowlers than some who are blessed with more natural talent. Why? Because they have applied themselves to the game. Bowling is one of those sports that looks *so* simple it is hard for some bowlers to appreciate that it is really more scientific than one might suspect. If you have an interest in improving your scores, or if you just want to build a fundamentally sound game, realize from the outset that it will take effort. One of the appeals of the sport is that bowlers can become involved as much or as minimally as they desire and can improve in accordance with how hard they are willing to work at it.

All bowlers have their own form, so don't be alarmed if you can't become picture-perfect. There are quite a few high-scoring bowlers who have quirks in their styles that seem to defy all the teaching they have absorbed. Somewhere along the way, though, most of these bowlers make up for their flawed styles by strengthening other parts of their game. Don Carter, considered by many to be the best bowler of all time, was a winner because he compensated for his hunchbacked delivery, maintaining excellent body balance. He also worked endlessly at his game, studied it, thought about it and practiced it.

27

Sooner or later all bowlers develop their own style. It may not look perfect, but with practice it should work.

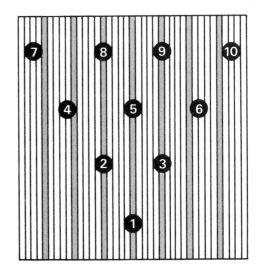

Each pin has a number, depending upon its location. An easy way to keep track of the pins is to remember that each of the four rows has one more pin in it than the row in front of it and that the numbering is always from left to right.

Bowling in the way that comes most naturally to you is the best way to start. Remember, though, that this is a sport of fundamental techniques and that the more fundamentally sound your game is, the better chance you will have of enjoying it and of rolling decent scores. So after you discover that your first tries leave something to be desired, study your form, think about what you do and then reason out how you can best improve various parts of your game through diligent practice. Many bowlers find that the best way to improve their game is to work on one phase of it at a time—pushaway, footwork, release, follow-through or whatever—until they have repaired it as best they can. Then they go on to another aspect of their game and work on that.

There is no better advice than to get some coaching from the local pro, who charges a fee for such lessons, or from a bowler you respect. They can study your form, determine what will be best for you and guide you through practice sessions in a way that you can get the most out of your time and talent.

Now for the fundamentals.

PICKING UP THE BALL

The first thing a bowler does when it is time to roll is to pick up the ball. That sounds so obvious that you might not give any thought to the procedure. A word of warning: Pick up the ball properly. No one can tell exactly when

Everyone can benefit from coaching. Here a young lady, helped by the guiding hand of a pro, learns a proper release.

Picking up the ball correctly will prevent fingers from being bruised by other balls as they return to the rack. Place your hands on the outside of the ball so there is no danger of being hit.

another ball is going to come whizzing onto the ball-return rack. Although it doesn't enter the rack with much speed, a ball doesn't stop until it bangs against another ball—or against someone's fingers. By placing your hands parallel to the rack, however, your fingers will be out of the way and, even if another ball hits yours, no damage will be done.

Some bowlers like to place their fingers in their ball while it's on the rack, then lift it off. This, too, is risky. More than a few bowlers have noticed a ball coming toward them, lifted their ball quickly without a tight grip and have had it thud to the floor or, worse yet, on their toes.

There is only one correct way to pick up the ball: Put one hand firmly on each side of the ball, get a good grip on it so it won't slip out of your hands, then lift the ball and cradle it in one arm and against your body. Now place your fingers in the ball. The index and middle fingers should go in first, then your thumb. Be sure your fingers always go in to the same depth.

YOUR AIMING PATTERN

On your first trip to a bowling center, notice the dark dots or arrows on the approaches and lanes. They may look decorative but they are there for a reason —to help you get lined up and to aim your shots. Each approach has dots or arrows with corresponding lane markers on the same board, and each set is spaced five boards apart. Using these as guidelines, you can learn to line up your

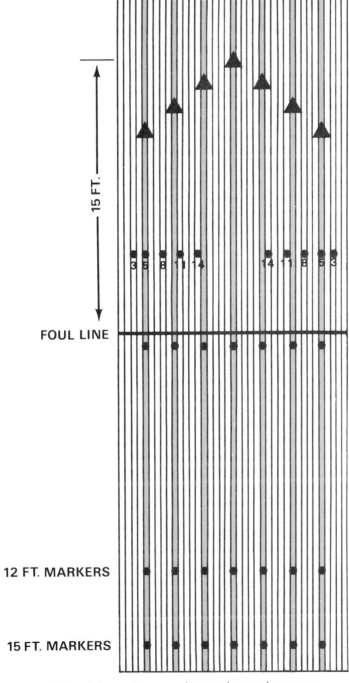

The dots and arrows located on a lane are uniformly placed and serve as checkpoints for your approach and targeting.

approach and to aim your ball on the same spots each time. (The lane markers will also help you to understand some of the terminology used by experienced bowlers. For instance, when a right-handed bowler says he is rolling his ball on the seventh board, he means he is rolling it two boards to the left of the first or outermost arrow.)

The approach, the sixteen-foot-long area behind the foul line, usually contains three sets of dots to help you to position your feet for your starting stance. Where you start is vital, but also learn to note where your feet finish up on the approach, where your sliding foot ends up when you are bowling your best. Then, when you get in a slump, you can check where your slide ends and see if you have drifted a few boards off to one side or the other. If so, you can adjust accordingly.

Two sets of seven markings each are placed on the lanes, one six to eight feet beyond the foul line, the other, twelve to sixteen feet down the lane. These markers can really help your game by acting as aiming aids, so keep an eye on them and figure out on what board your ball lands and what boards it rolls over on the way to the pins.

Lane dots (above), forward of the foul line by 6 to 8 feet, are placed on boards 3, 5, 8, 11 and 14 from either edge.

Targeting arrows (left) are located approximately 15 feet forward of the foul line and are 5 boards apart.

TARGETING TECHNIQUES

Novice bowlers often have two assumptions—that the objective of the game is to knock down all 10 pins and that the way to accomplish this is to roll the ball so it will hit the front pin (headpin) flush on. The first notion is correct: The ultimate is to fell all 10 pins with the first shot and thereby score what's called a strike. But the second assumption is false because, in most cases, a head-on hit will not provide enough of what is called "mixing" to bring down all the pins. The surest way to get a strike is to roll the ball into the "pocket" between the 1 and 3 pins for a right-hander and between the 1 and 2 pins for a left-hander. Not only that, the goal is to deliver the ball into the pocket at precisely the right angle.

Most bowlers use one of four basic targeting techniques to aim their delivery at the pocket. They are called pin, spot, line, and area bowling.

Pin Bowling

Those who use this technique merely fix their eyes on the pins, normally selecting the 1-3 strike pocket as their objective. But it's a long way from release point to the pins, and for many, aiming at a target sixty feet away is not easy. To be an effective pin bowler you must draw an imaginary line from the point of release to the target spot so that you will have a precise idea of the path your ball should take.

Spot Bowling

Spot bowling is based on the theory that it is easier to hit a target a few feet away than one many feet distant. Instead of aiming for the strike pocket sixty feet down the lane, the bowler picks a target on the line to the strike pocket and aims for that point. The target may be at the foul line or farther down the lane. Most bowlers use the arrows embedded in the lanes, but other aids can help. Whatever you use, just be sure you have an imaginary line from start to finish and pick your spot somewhere along the line. But remember: Hitting the target spot doesn't guarantee a good roll. Consistency is critical. You must do the same thing each time, from approach to release, to ensure that hitting the spot will put the ball on target. In both pin and spot bowling, it is imperative to keep your eye on the pin or target until the ball is released.

Pin Bowling

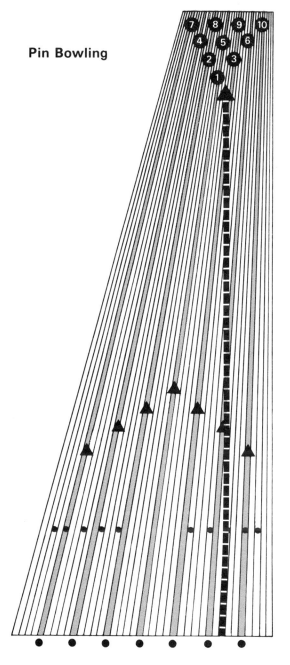

Spot Bowling

This method is both simple and difficult. What makes it easy is that the eyes are focused on the pins, usually the 1–3 pocket, throughout the approach—something that comes naturally to many people. What makes pin bowling hard is that the target is so far down the lane.

Some bowlers find that the easiest targeting technique is to aim at a close-in object—a dot near the foul line or an arrow on the lane. To help you settle on a target, it is best to envision the desired trajectory of your shot and then to pick a spot somewhere along that imaginary line.

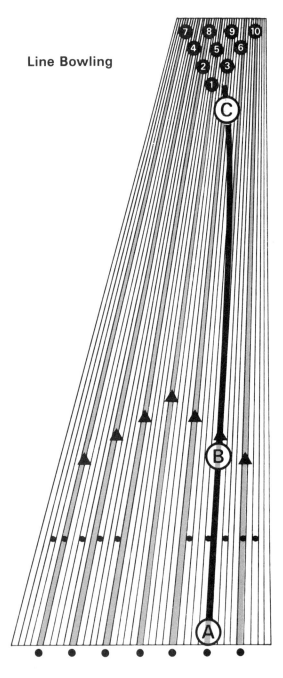

Line Bowling

Area Bowling

This is a combination of pin and spot bowling. Although there are variations on this technique, most line bowling is done by focusing on a spot near the foul line (A), shifting the eyes to a second target on the lane (B) and then glancing at the strike pocket (C) just before releasing the ball.

Here the objective is to aim in the vicinity of one of the arrows on the lane. This target zone should include the arrow and one board on either side of it, a technique that takes away much of the strain that bowlers feel when aiming at a smaller object.

Line Bowling

Line bowling could be called a combination of spot and pin bowling. Here again the bowler checks his imaginary line of delivery, but establishes a variety of checkpoints along his so-called line. He may use any or all of the targets: starting spot, a spot at the foul line, spots on the lane, and the pins.

Area Bowling

Most bowlers are area bowlers. Although they select a spot or a line, they are more than satisfied if they can roll to within a board of each side of the target. Although the area bowler may not be as accurate as the true spot bowler, he usually finds it easier to hit the target area because he is more relaxed. And hitting anywhere close to the target area will usually result in a ball around the pocket.

Try all four targeting techniques, find out which works for you and then stick with it. Although it is generally agreed that the spot method is best, consistency is the real key.

To determine your starting point, begin with your back to the foul line and your heels a few inches from the stripe, then pace off 4½ quick steps (A). Turn around (B) and roll a few shots to see whether you need to adjust your takeoff point backward or forward.

A

B

5

The Approach

To determine where to begin your approach, stand with your back to the pins, your heels about two inches from the foul line. Then take 4½ brisk steps toward the seating area, make an about-face and check where your feet are in reference to the dots on the approach surface. Use this spot as a takeoff point, no matter how many steps you take during your delivery. After you have rolled several balls you'll know whether you should adjust your takeoff point. If your slide takes you beyond the foul line, move the starting point back. If you come up short, move it forward.

To determine your lateral position on the lane, line up your right shoulder with the second dot to the right of center on the approach. Now you will also be in line with the second arrow or tenth board on the lane, generally considered the best target area for a strike ball. For those who use three, five or seven steps, the same general principles apply. (All the instructions in this book are for right-handers, but left-handers can easily put them to use by substituting left for right.)

THE STANCE

O.K., we're ready to go. Standing at your takeoff point with your fingers in the ball holes, use your right hand to raise the ball forward to the most natural and comfortable position for you to hold it, making sure it is not above your shoulder level or below the waist. Keep your right wrist firm and place your left hand under the ball to carry most of its weight. The higher you hold the ball, the more speed you will be able to generate, but remember: Don't overdo it, since speed is not all that important in knocking down pins. Whether you hold the ball close to your body or a little out front is up to you. More important is keeping the right elbow tucked in close to the hip and the ball slightly off to the right so that you will have a clear path for your armswing. If you have large hips, just move the ball farther to the right.

Now, while holding the ball, try to picture it as a clock facing you, with twelve at the top, six o'clock at the bottom, three to the right and nine to the left. With this image in mind, position your thumb at eleven o'clock (for left-handers, one o'clock). Another gimmick to help keep your thumb in the proper spot is to think of it as being in the same position as when you shake hands.

At this point, you should be in a relaxed, standing position, perhaps leaning forward a bit if it is more comfortable. Both shoulders should be level and squared to your target. Your knees, at least your right one, should be bent just a trifle. If you are using a four-step delivery, place your left foot a little forward and shift some or most of your weight to it.

Now that you are ready to start into motion, fix your eyes on your target area. Concentrate and relax. If you are tense, your timing and rhythm will be thrown off and you will have difficulty bowling smoothly. If you have trouble staying loose, a deep breath will often be enough to relax you. If that doesn't work, lower the ball, back off from your starting position and then, when you are ready, resume your stance.

There are plenty of little things to remember about preparing to bowl, but they are all so simple that with practice they will soon become automatic. Practice is the key. And what has been outlined so far can be practiced without even rolling a ball. Just step up on the approach and, as long as you are not interfering with other bowlers, get your stance down pat, with or without a ball. You can even practice this at home in front of a mirror—a full-length one, if available—so that you can look at yourself from head to toe, head-on and from both sides. Look for the following checkpoints in your stance:

Once you have settled on a starting point, make a mental note of exactly where your feet are positioned so that you can line up on the same spot each time. These dots, located near the back of the approach area, should become your reference points.

In the ideal stance, the left foot should be slightly ahead of the right, the knees bent a bit and the elbows at the sides. The shoulders should be squared and the eyes focused on a target.

A B

1. Upright, relaxed posture.
2. Eyes on target.
3. Shoulders level and squared to target.
4. Most of ball weight in the left hand.
5. Right wrist straight and firm.
6. Thumb at eleven o'clock (one o'clock for left-handers).
7. Ball held slightly to the right.
8. Elbow close to hip.
9. Knees relaxed.
10. Feet close together, the left one a few inches forward.

Get these items down pat and it will make the rest of your game easier. You may wish to alter some of the steps, which is fine. Feel free to make adjustments as the need or whim arises. The more you experiment, the sooner you will be able to settle on a stance that is best tailored for you. You may find that you can roll higher scores by starting off with the ball held under your chin. Or that holding the ball at arm's length at your side is ideal. There are fine bowlers, even some professionals, who use such methods. Don't be afraid to experiment. It is part of the fun of bowling.

Thrusting the ball out slightly helps begin a smooth approach (A). A pushaway that is too extended (B) and too high or one that is too low (C) can cause problems with timing as the approach continues.

c

Now that you're settled on your stance, let's get on with the approach. Many insist that it is the most important part of the game. Pro bowler Patty Costello states, "If you don't get to the foul line the right way, you can't possibly release the ball correctly. Your follow-through, your aim, your balance and your score will suffer."

You've picked up the ball, positioned yourself on the approach in a comfortable stance and have settled on an aiming technique. It is time to start rolling. Since most bowlers use a four-step delivery (actually three steps and a slide), we will use this as the basis of our instruction. After each step is described, a quick checklist will be provided so you can quickly tick off what is involved in each.

Step One

Your first step forward is known as the "pushaway." Begin it only when you are relaxed and satisfied that you are concentrating on your target. Most bowlers do not take a step here, preferring to shuffle forward without lifting their foot off the floor. However you do it, this step should be the shortest of the four, somewhere between twelve and eighteen inches. Don't rush. There is no advantage to getting to the foul line faster than a speeding bullet.

Simultaneous with the first step come two other movements: a bending forward of the body and a pushing away of the ball to a point just ahead of the right foot. As with all phases of the approach, the pushing away of the ball should be smooth and unhurried. Even though this is called the pushaway, the movement should be far less than a push. You want just to nudge the ball into position so that it can swing easily.

Near the end of step one, the left hand starts to leave the ball or, as many bowlers find, has already left the ball. While all this is going on, your right wrist should be firm, your shoulders squared to the target and your eyes on your target.

1. Bend forward slightly.
2. Move the right foot straight forward 12 to 18 inches.
3. Push the ball forward and to the right.
4. Left hand leaves or starts to leave the ball.
5. Right wrist firm.
6. Shoulders parallel to target.
7. Eyes on target.

Step Two

The important elements in this part of the approach concern the left foot and the right arm. Once you have begun your approach, it is easy to drift—that is, to wander from side to side with your second, third and fourth steps. If your second step, your left-foot step, drifts to the left, you will most likely compensate by drifting to the right on your third step and then back to the left on your slide. Such wobbling will ruin your entire delivery, so make certain that your second step is taken straight ahead and not off to the side. It is also imperative that you keep your right arm close to your body as you bring the ball back.

Step two ends with the ball, which will be carried back by its own weight and momentum, swinging through a straight-down position with the arm fully extended. While the right arm is down, the left arm should be going up and away from the body to provide the balance necessary to prevent drifting.

To repeat:

1. Step straight ahead with left foot.
2. Right arm straight, swinging close to body.
3. Left arm moves up and to the side.
4. Eyes on target.

Step Three

You should accelerate a little during step three, made with your right foot. Be careful that you do this smoothly and without any sudden or herky-jerky motion. While thrusting the right foot straight ahead, the body should lean forward. Let the ball continue to swing back under its own power. At the conclusion of step three, the ball will reach the peak of its backswing, not more than shoulder high, in most cases considerably lower. Keep the armswing straight by maintaining a firm wrist. Finish up with the left knee bent and with the right foot firmly planted.

Again:

1. Don't rush. The most common mistake here is to rush one or more parts of the body. As with all phases of the approach, keep all movements smooth and unhurried.

2. Accelerate slightly and smoothly.

3. Step straight forward with right foot.

4. Lean forward.

5. Straight armswing.

6. Right wrist firm.

7. Right knee bent.

8. Eyes on target.

Step Four

During your third step, you generated power by pushing off with the right foot and by thrusting your body forward. Most of the work in step four will be done by the left leg and foot. As the left foot slides straight ahead toward the foul line, the knee should be bent to prepare for the delivery of the ball onto the lane. Your slide on the leather sole is stopped by a transfer of weight to the rubber heel on the left shoe. As the left foot approaches the foul line, the right arm brings the ball to its release point.

How much you bend at the waist and how much you bend the left knee depend largely upon your style. The primary purpose of bending is to lower the ball so that the point of release will be low enough to avoid excessive lofting of the ball. If you are not down low enough, the ball will sail well down the lane before it unceremoniously thuds to the boards.

Four Step Delivery

A B   C

G   H   I

A relaxed stance, with the ball chest high, elbows tucked in and eyes on target (A) is essential at the beginning of any delivery. The pushaway (B) is initiated by nudging the ball slightly away from the body and taking a short step with the right foot. As the left foot takes the second step (C), the ball begins its descent and the right knee is bent to prepare for the third step (D). The right arm is straight, the eyes are still on target and the left arm swings out to provide balance as the right foot starts to come up (E). To provide balance, the left arm is thrust farther to the side, the right foot lands straight ahead, knees are bent

D E   F

J K   L

and the ball glides back on a straight path (F). When the ball nears the peak of its backswing, the right foot carries most of the weight as the left foot poises for the final step (G). At the top of the backswing, the left foot should be firmly planted, the left arm fully extended and the ball of the right foot should lend support (H). During the slide toward the foul line, the ball begins its forward swing (I). By keeping the right arm firm and by maintaining a straight-ahead slide (J), a smooth release is possible (K). An automatic follow-through and a balanced finish (L) conclude the delivery.

48 If you have difficulty getting the waist down and leaning, it may well be because your slide is too short. The farther you extend the left leg forward and the right leg back, the lower your waist will automatically be. Don't be surprised if your left leg aches when you try to lengthen your slide. At the end of the slide, it is bearing all the body weight, and it takes time to become accustomed to this, time for your muscles to become strong enough to withstand the strain.

Perfect timing will bring the left foot and the extended right arm to the foul line at the same instant. The ball is released as it passes the left foot. At this point, the right wrist and arm should be fairly firm and straight. The thumb must still be in its original eleven-o'clock position. Both the left arm and the right foot are extended for balance. The finishing of both will depend on what feels comfortable. After the release comes the follow-through. With your eyes still on the target area, continue your upward swing of the arm to at least waist level, possibly as high as your chin. Delivery complete, step back to admire the movement of your ball as it rolls down the lane and goes to work on the pins.

1. Push forward off right foot.
2. Slide on front of left foot.
3. Bend left knee.
4. Bend at the waist and lean forward.
5. Let the ball swing forward under its own momentum.
6. Right wrist and arm fairly straight.
7. Thumb at 11 o'clock; 1 o'clock for left-handers.
8. Continue to bend left knee as left foot slides to a stop.
9. Finish slide a few inches from the foul line.
10. Left foot pointed straight ahead.
11. Release ball across foul line.
12. Left arm and right foot extended for balance.
13. Watch those pins fall down.

OTHER DELIVERIES

The Five-Step Delivery

In any delivery where more than four steps will be used, the key is to work them around the basic four-step approach. For example, in the five-step delivery a bowler would simply take a short step before moving the ball at all. Once that step is taken, the rest boils down to being a four-step approach. If more than five steps are taken, the same thing is recommended: Hold the ball in place during the extra steps and then swing into the four-step delivery. (Some bowlers prefer to start out by holding the ball well out in front, then bring it back toward the body during their first step.) Experienced bowlers who find that they are rushing their shots and can't seem to overcome this tendency sometimes use an extra step or two or even three to slow themselves down.

The Three-Step Delivery

The three-step delivery is a different, much quicker movement. It is used by those who find that the faster they move through their approach, the higher their scores go. Here the left foot and the ball must move out swiftly because, in effect, the pushaway and downswing of the four-step delivery are combined. The last two steps of the three-step are then the same as those used for a four-step approach.

All sorts of other deliveries can be used—even the old one-step, employed so successfully by the late Count Gengler. Gengler, who came over from Germany early in the twentieth century and became one of the most legendary bowlers of all time, used only one step because he felt that the less movement there was in the approach, the less chance there would be to make mistakes. He stepped forward, planted his left foot near the foul line, bent his right knee as he brought the ball forward and then followed through. Gengler was so proficient that he once bowled with all the lights in the lanes turned off. On that memorable occasion, the lights were turned on only long enough for him to pick up his ball and go back to his starting point on the approach. Then the lights were flicked off. Twelve times Gengler rolled. Twelve times he got a strike— a 300 game. The lean and lanky Gengler not only bowled differently, he also dressed uniquely, always wearing a tie and vest while bowling. And he often used a ball without finger holes. Few, if any bowlers, were more consistent than Count Gengler.

Five Step Delivery

A B   C

G H   I

No matter how many steps are used, the essentials of all deliveries are the same. The only thing that distinguishes the five-step from the four-step is the extra step at the outset, a getting-underway maneuver that some bowlers find to be most comfortable and natural. All bowlers have their own traits. Here the bowler takes his stance with the ball held waist high (A). In the five-step, the first movement is made with the left foot rather than the right (B). Once in motion, there is more danger of veering off to one side or the other, but a straight-ahead second step and an on-line pushaway (C) will

D E F

J K

prevent that. Eyes must be on a target (D) and the right arm straight through-out the backswing as the left foot comes up (E). A forward lean from the waist up (F), plus a solidly placed fourth step and thrust-out left arm (G), lend balance. As the left foot slides into the fifth step (H), the ball comes forward, the straight arm (I) carrying it to the point of release (J). When the left foot has braked to a stop just short of the foul line, everything should be in balance: left arm and right leg extended, left knee bent and right arm winding up the follow-through (K).

The only real variation between the the four- and the five-step approach is that one short step is taken to get the four-step under way (left), while two are used in the five-step (right).

Three Step Delivery

A   B   C

After the pushaway (A), the bowler takes a lengthy first step as he begins to bring the ball back (B). As he continues his backswing, the bowler lowers his body (C), thrusts his left arm out for balance and launches into his second step. Eaglelike, the bowler reaches the top of his backswing while maintaining perfect balance (D). With his eyes always on the target, the bowler keeps

D E   F

his shoulders squared and his armswing straight throughout the third step (E).
All the ingredients are here for a happy ending (F): straight-ahead slide,
straight follow-through, left arm and right leg extended to provide balance
while gliding forward on the left foot. Even if you do not use a three-step,
all these essentials must be incorporated into whatever approach you do use.

The Release

Despite the brevity of it, the moment of release is one of the most critical and fascinating aspects of bowling. Everything you have done during the approach has led up to this instant. From here on, much of what happens to the ball will be determined by how the fingers are removed from the ball.

So let's examine what takes place during the last phase. There is much more to it than simply letting the ball go. In sequence, the release is made up of three elements: (1) *where* the ball is released; (2) the *direction* in which the ball is released; and (3) *how* the ball is released.

As you might suspect, where the ball is released and the direction of its release are the least complicated facets of this process. But don't think that they are less important than how the ball is sent on its way. For the release to be correct, each aspect of it must be performed just so.

RELEASE POINT

To avoid excessive lift, the ball must be released below the level of the left knee. Professional bowler Nelson (Bo) Burton, Jr., insists, "The big

Executed properly, the release is a brief but all-important phase of bowling. The thumb will come out of the ball hole first and then lift is applied by the fingers. This gives the ball varying amounts of spin, which cause it to hook, curve or back up.

secret to a good bowling game is the location of the ball at the point of release. The release point of each shot should be consistently in a position near the sliding foot, just in front of the ankle. This is necessary to get leverage. It doesn't take a physically strong person to release an accurate, effective shot—provided those muscles that are in use are used properly. If the ball is more than a few inches away from the sliding foot during the release, the bowler will not be able to get his body into the shot, and even the arm will be inhibited from guiding the ball freely to the spot." At the instant of release, the toe of the left (sliding) foot will be only a few inches from the foul line. After release, the ball will sail across the foul stripe.

FINGER RELEASE

In order for the ball to be sent careening down the lane, the index finger, ring finger and thumb must obviously be removed from the ball. Cartoonists have had fun with what may transpire if the fingers don't come out of the ball at all. Yes, most of these cartoons are farfetched, but many bowlers can attest to embarrassing moments when their fingers have been reluctant to come out of the finger holes. What generally happens is that the ball sails through the air, describing an arc more desirable to shotputting than to bowling.

Why the difficulty in release? The fingers—and the thumb in particular— tend to swell after rolling for a while and they sometimes get hung up in the ball. To make room for the swollen thumb, bowlers place several layers of tape inside the thumb hole before starting and then periodically remove one or more of the layers as a bowling session wears on. Even the most skilled professionals occasionally will have trouble, however. Palmer Fallgren can testify to that, for what happened to him has become one of the most famous tales on the PBA tour. Fallgren's fingers came out of the ball so late that his ball went almost straight up, not altering its flight until it struck the ceiling with a resounding thud. This took place during a PBA tournament at the Madison Square Garden lanes where, if nothing else, Fallgren left a mark that will probably never be topped.

So much for the improbable. It is time to get down to the subject at hand —namely, how your release will determine the track of the ball and the type of shot you will have.

SLIDE, ROLL AND HOOK

If you have not already done so, spend some time at a bowling center watching the way a ball goes down the lane. What you see may surprise you. Most newcomers to the sport, and even some who have been around for a while, believe that a bowling ball does nothing more than roll down the lane. By watching, however, you will soon discover that the ball does far more than that.

To begin, understand that only the first thirty to forty feet of the lane beyond the foul stripe—the hardwood section—are oiled. This makes it easy to understand why a ball skids when it lands. No oil is applied to the remainder of the lane. Lacking adequate friction, the ball will continue to slide or skid until it reaches the unoiled softwood section. At that point, the ball will finally attain enough traction to start rolling. Then, in the case of all bowlers except those who throw a truly straight shot, the ball will enter the third and final phase of its path to the pins. During this last portion, which will cover between fifteen and twenty feet, the ball should suddenly hook toward the strike pocket.

The hook, which brings the ball into the strike pocket at the sharpest possible angle, is the best all-around shot. An explanation of why the hook is so effective will come later. First, though, it will be better to take a look at what is known as the "track" of the ball.

BALL TRACK

After you have been rolling your bowling ball for a while, you will notice that it has begun to wear what might be described as a "collar." This circular pattern, which is most often referred to as the track, has been put on the ball by its roll across the surface of the lane. If you run your fingers across the track, you will feel the slight amount of oil and grit that the ball has picked up. You will also see and feel that the collar is actually becoming grooved into the ball as some of the glossy finish on the ball wears off. The track or collar will give you clues about exactly how you are releasing your shot and whether you are throwing a full roller, a semi-roller or a spinner, the three most common types of roll. It will aid you in determining how you are manipulating your hand, wrist and arm, and will also show whether or not you are getting your fingers out of the ball the way you had hoped to.

A

B

The rotation of the fingers during the release will determine the type of roll a ball has. On the full roller (A), the track on the ball will be around the entire circumference of the ball, usually between the thumb hole and the finger holes. A semi-roller's collar (B) will be worn slightly below the thumb hole. On the spinner (C), the track will be even farther below the thumb hole.

C

THE SEMI-ROLLER

The semi-roller is used by a majority of bowlers. Its popularity comes from the fact that it remains consistent on almost all lane conditions as well as providing a sharp-breaking hook shot. On the semi-roller, the track is almost always below and to the left of the thumb hole.

To throw a semi-roller, keep the wrist straight during the release, while turning the forearm counterclockwise. Don't fret if you bend your wrist slightly and are scoring well. But bowl a few balls with a straight wrist just to find out if you get even better results. If it does not help, go back to your natural way of doing things. The finger that will apply most of the turn on the semi-roller will be the ring finger, which will come out of the ball last.

If you are using a semi and are not getting sufficient mixing action among the pins, check the collar on the ball. It can give you a clue to what you are doing wrong. If the collar is more than two inches from the thumb hole, you are making a mistake common to those who throw a semi-roller—overturning the ball. Too much counterclockwise force is being applied to the ball by the forearm and fingers. Reduce the turning and you'll have more mixing among the pins and, best of all, higher scores.

Thumb position is critical. Overturning will result if there is too much variation in the thumb position during the forward swing. If the thumb is as far right as three o'clock when you start to turn the ball, then it should be no farther left than eleven o'clock at release. How can you tell exactly what your thumb is doing during the release? It's difficult, so ask another bowler to watch the position of your thumb from the height of your backswing, during the forward swing and, most importantly, during the turn and release.

THE FULL ROLLER

The full roller, so called because it wears its track around the full circumference of the ball, is a popular roll because it has a strong mixing action as it strikes the pins. For a full roller, the thumb is usually at or close to nine o'clock at the height of the backswing, and depending on one's own particular style, will wind up anywhere from two o'clock to twelve o'clock at the point of release. The closer the thumb is to twelve o'clock, the more effective the full roller will be because it will have been given more of a counterclockwise turn and will finish with more hook.

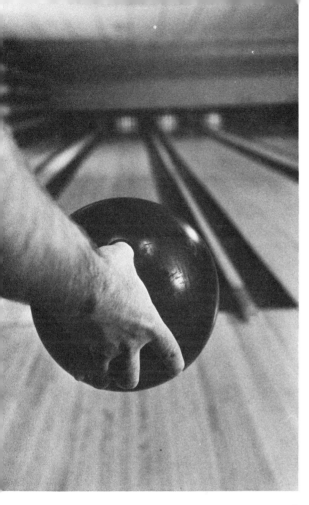

A

It is important to be aware of where your thumb is at the instant of release. To achieve this, most bowlers think in terms of the ball being a clock. For example, bowlers whose hook shots are not breaking properly can often correct the problem after noticing that they are releasing the ball with the thumb outside the desired position between ten o'clock and eleven o'clock. Here the thumb is at twelve o'clock (A) and at ten o'clock (B).

B

THE SPINNER

For a spinner, even more of a counterclockwise turn is given to the ball. The thumb shifts from about three o'clock at the top of the backswing to as far as ten o'clock at release. Applying that much twist makes it difficult for most bowlers to give the ball the lift that is needed, and it requires considerable strength. But with proper lift, the spinner will result in a wickedly big hook, a shot that was highly effective years ago but that has lost much of its punch because of today's lighter pins and slicker lane conditions. On the spinner, the collar will cover only a small fraction of the ball below the thumb hole.

THE FOUR BASIC SHOTS

All the various types of rolls result, in one way or another, in specific shots, the most basic of which include the following: the straight ball, the hook ball, the curve ball and the backup ball. The names of these shots describe the path of their forward motion as opposed to the previously mentioned roll of the ball.

The Straight Ball

As we look at the various shots, picture, if you will, how each enters the strike pocket and what happens to the pins. A straight ball travels, as one might suspect, in a relatively straight line and will be subject to considerable deflection, since it will tend to shove its way through the pins. Therefore, a straight ball that enters the pocket at anything other than the precisely perfect spot (the right side of the headpin) is not likely to result in a strike. If the No. 1 pin is hit too flush, it will sail straight back into the No. 5 and won't fulfill one of its main functions, starting a domino effect to wipe out the right side—the Nos. 3, 6 and 10 pins. If the headpin is hit right on the nose, it will probably take out the 5, which is directly behind it. But the 5 would then continue straight back and go right between the 8 and 9 pins. If the headpin is hit too lightly, the opposite will often take place: The No. 1 pin will not knock down all, or sometimes any, of the left-side pins. Nothing has been mentioned yet about the middle three pins—Nos. 5, 8 and 9. If No. 3 is hit squarely, it would have a good chance of felling the No. 9, but it would not take out the 5 or the 8. Obviously, the straight shot isn't a high-percentage shot.

The Hook Ball

Now for the hook shot. If you have a natural hook, stick with it. It is a very effective shot, since it allows for more margin of error than the straight ball. Strikes can be picked up with hook shots that are not quite perfect, a luxury seldom enjoyed by those who roll a straight shot. The hook of the ball comes from the lifting motion of the middle and ring fingers during the release, and the prime reason it is so effective is the somewhat mysterious mixing action it generates among the pins. When the hook shot glances off the Nos. 1, 3 and 5 pins, it will upend them somewhat differently than a straight ball. Instead of being merely driven back, pins will be inclined to fall slightly sideways as they go back. Once tilted in this manner, they will take up more space during their flight and, as a result, will be more likely to crash into other pins than those that go back in a more erect manner.

The Curve Ball

In throwing the curve, actually an exaggerated hook, the arm and wrist will be turned to the left, and the thumb will generally come out of the ball at about nine o'clock. Its wide circling path makes it hard to control but, if it crashes into the strike pocket just right, it can sweep away all 10 pins. Should it not enter the pocket properly, however, all sorts of leaves are possible. At its worst, a big-bending curve will sweep behind the headpin without even touching it. At its best, the curve ball will enter the strike pocket at enough of an angle so that the pins will mix well, taking out other pins.

The Backup Ball

Last *and* least is the backup ball. Avoid it. Instead of breaking *into* the 1-3 pocket, the backup ball will break *away* from it. If it is your natural shot and you find you are unable to adapt to another one, move to the left side of the approach and aim the ball over the second arrow from the left. That way, since the backup breaks from left to right, it will break into the 1-2 strike area normally used by left-handers. In a way, the backup is like the screwball thrown by baseball pitchers. But whereas the pitcher can often befuddle batters with this form of reverse curve, the pins cannot be similarly baffled. So stow the backup. Work on turning the ball from right to left (counterclockwise) rather than from left to right. Join the hookers.

The Four Basic Shots

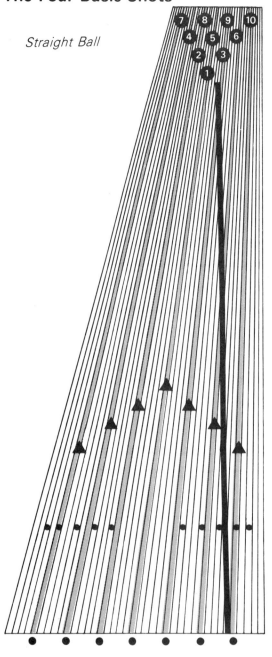

Straight Ball

It is far better to roll this shot close to the second arrow than down the center of the lane, since it will have a better chance of entering the strike pocket and getting good mixing action among the pins.

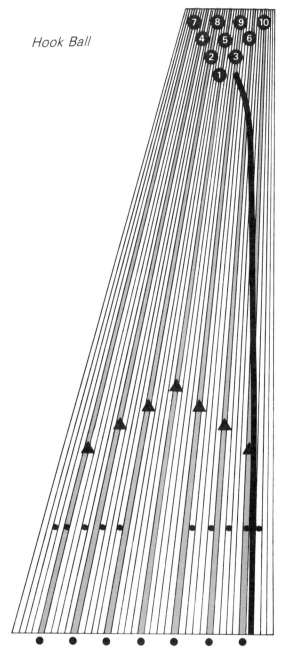

Hook Ball

This is the most consistent strike-getter for most bowlers. A well-thrown hook will set up chain reactions on both sides—the 1, 2, 4 and 7 pins on the left and the 3, 6 and 10 on the right. The ball will then hit the 5, which will take care of the 8 and deflect into the 9.

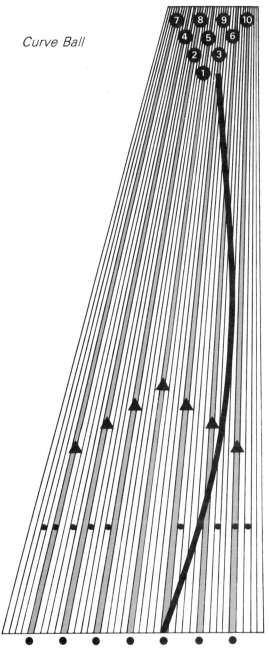

Curve Ball

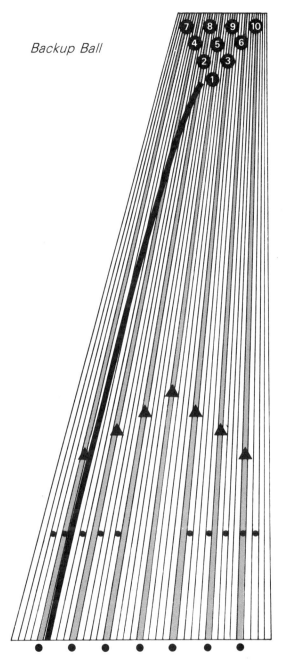

Backup Ball

Control is the hard-to-master secret of this wide-sweeping shot. Two things make this difficult to achieve: 1) it is necessary to apply more lift to the curve ball than to the hook; and 2) the wide path of the shot leaves more room for error.

Instead of breaking from right to left as the hook does, this rarely used shot breaks the opposite way. Some bowlers who use the backup ball aim it to the right of center, but generally it is best to start on the far left of the approach and aim for the second arrow on that side.

THE PERFECT STRIKE

The best route to a perfect strike is a good hook shot. The angle of the hook is the key to its success. To visualize a textbook strike, picture the ball making its first contact with the pins by breaking sharply into the 1-3 pocket and hitting the right side of the headpin. Executed properly, the ball will *not* hit the headpin squarely. Striking the No. 1 pin flush is referred to as a "high" hit and will move the headpin back on a path that is too straight. By hitting the right side of the No. 1 pin, it will force it back at an angle. The headpin should start a domino reaction among the pins on that side. The No. 1 pin will hit the No. 2 pin, which will be driven back against the No. 4 pin, which will take out the No. 7. That's the end of the left side of the rack of pins. So far, the ball has made contact with only one pin. Upon striking the headpin, the ball—even though it weighs as much as sixteen pounds and is rolling with force—will be deflected slightly to the right. Perfect. This puts the ball in position to hit the left side of the No. 3 pin and set a chain reaction on the right side. Like the No. 1 pin, the No. 3 will not go straight back, but will fly at an angle so that it will topple the 6 pin. When it is knocked backward, the No. 6 pin will wipe out the 10 pin. That's the end of the right side. Seven pins down. Three to go.

Now for the pesky three pins in the middle: Nos. 5, 8 and 9. On this perfect strike, the ball will be deflected a teeny bit to the left by the No. 3 pin and will send No. 5 veering off slightly to the left to take out the 8 pin. Then the ball will conclude its work by polishing off the 9 pin.

Let's review. Improbable as it may at first seem, the ball will hit only four pins during its zigzag course. Each of the four will be struck with less force and, logically enough, each will do less work than the previous one. One of these pins—the headpin—will take out three others (Nos. 2, 4 and 7). The No. 3 pin will take care of two others (Nos. 6 and 10). And the 5 pin will sweep away the 8. The only pin that does not have to take out another is No. 9.

This is the *perfect strike.* Many, many times strikes are achieved in other ways. Pins sometimes rebound off the side or rear walls, fly back onto the lane and bring down other pins. Or the pins will twist, turn and clatter about and a strike will result. But this theoretically perfect strike with its combination of pin and ball action is the surest way of knocking down all 10 pins.

If you are finding the mechanics of the release hard to understand, don't worry—you're in good company. Listen to the words Carmen Salvino, one of only a few men who are members of both the ABC and the PBA Halls of Fame: "I doubt that anyone in the world fully understands the release. Maybe we

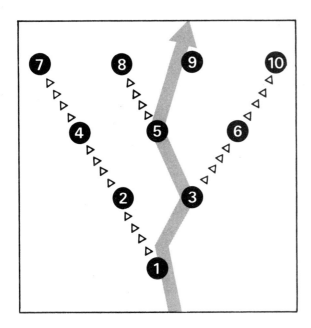

On a "perfect strike," the ball will hit only four pins. The remaining pins will be toppled by a series of chain reactions among them.

could if somehow we could see the inside of the ball and all that is going on within it. . . . But all I can say is that even after all my years on the lanes, I am *still* learning about it. The release takes just a fraction of a second, but *so much* happens during that instant. Even though it is so complex and so quick, the release is something that all bowlers should study and try to understand as best they can."

68

Economy of movement characterizes Carmen Salvino's approach to bowling. His upright follow-through may appear unorthodox but it's simple and it works.

A COMMENT ON THE FOLLOW-THROUGH

You may wonder why little has been said yet about the follow-through. Quite frankly, it is because we don't attach a lot of importance to the follow-through. To quote Carmen Salvino again, "The follow-through is a fallacy. There is nothing wrong with it, mind you. It's just that if you do everything else well, it will be virtually impossible *not* to follow through." How true. Or at least so it seems to us. After all, once the ball has been released, it's on its way, and the completion of your motion can't affect it. Yet some bowlers swear that it is one of the most vital segments of their game and, if their follow-through does not end with their hand in front of their face or even as far back as the top of their head, they feel they have committed a grave mistake. That does not seem logical, though. Once the ball and you have parted company, it will not matter how vigorously you follow through with your hand, for the ball is on its own with its course, its track and its mixing action already established.

A good follow-through will be the result of a well-executed approach and will begin with the arm swinging on a straight line right through the release point (A) and extending up to about eye level (B).

A

B

7

Mastering the Basics

The next time you go to the lanes, study the form of the bowlers. Undoubtedly you will see droves of men and women, boys and girls who have never mastered the basics. You won't have much trouble spotting their flaws: big hitches in the armswing, wandering feet, off-balance slides to the foul line and much more. Some of these people may be only occasional bowlers, not interested in sharpening their skills and raising their scores. Others will be regulars who for any number of reasons have never really cared to improve, people content to roll the same scores week after week. If they only knew how easy it is to polish up their techniques and to add at least a few pins to the scores, many of them would take the time to master the basics. If you are willing to do that, you are almost guaranteed of getting more enjoyment out of the game than those who have not.

Let's look closely at the approach, dissecting and analyzing each phase. Read these details carefully. Read them—study them—thoroughly and thoughtfully. There is a difference between bowling and *knowing* how to bowl. The more you know about the various components of the game, how and why they should function, how they mesh with one another, the more you will be able to correct and improve your game to get the maximum scores and most fun out of the sport.

MENTAL PREPARATION

Even before arriving at the lanes, you should get yourself in the proper frame of mind to bowl. Be ready. Think success. Everyone should have a good time at the lanes, but don't get so caught up in the camaraderie and storytelling that you become distracted from your game. While waiting your turn to roll, think about what you are going to do once you get on the approach. Picture how to correct problems you may have been having lately. Think positively. Imagine yourself rolling at your best. Once you begin your delivery, everything should be instinctive. The more advance thought you have given to how you will perform, the more spontaneous and effective will be your roll.

While on the approach, lock your concentration on the target. Bowlers are usually taught to remain motionless for the few moments before takeoff time. Many a fine bowler, however, finds it helps to move a bit in order to remain loose, perhaps finger-tapping the ball or using a slight rocking motion. They get these movements down to a rhythmic cadence, at the end of which they automatically launch into their delivery. Others count to themselves or think of a pet phrase. Then, on whatever is their magic number or trigger word, they begin their roll.

THE PUSHAWAY

One of the novice bowler's most common mistakes is to use too much force to nudge the ball into motion. Instead of gently moving the ball forward and off to the right so that the arm and the ball will easily drop into the downswing, they shove the ball upward, often so high that it looks like they're playing basketball. Right from the start, their timing will be way out of sync. Eliminate the upward shove and you will simplify your approach; simplicity is one of the bywords of the game. Bowling is a highly logical sport, and there is no logical reason for pushing the ball up when the objective is to have it go down.

However, if you determine that you need a higher or a lower backswing, the place to make such an adjustment is during the pushaway—not, as many suspect, by trying to add to or to take away from the swing of the arm. To increase the height of the backswing, it is best to put a tiny bit more oomph into the pushaway. Conversely, to cut down on the height of the backswing, the thing to do is to slow down on the first step.

Remember, the pushaway consists of far more than nudging the ball into position. Your first step is critical. Take your time. Those pins aren't going anywhere—until your ball hits them. Glide through that first step, making certain your weight is balanced as you move. It will take some practice to find out how long your first step should be, but it should be shorter than any of the others. If you find that you are rushing through the rest of your approach, the odds are that your first step is too short to get you into gear. If your last three steps are too slow (much less likely), then you should try a first step that is a little longer.

OBEY THE SPEED LIMIT

Many male bowlers seem to believe that they can prove their virility by firing the ball down the lane with all their might. Some women, too, fling the ball with all their strength, believing that they can overpower the pins. About the only thing they are going to prove by doing that is that might is not right. Dick Weber and Mrs. Floretta McCutcheon, regarded by many as the finest male and

Floretta McCutcheon was one of the greatest women bowlers even though she rolled the seldom-used "backup" ball (notice her hand position at release, which imparted a left-to-right roll to the ball). So outstanding was her game that she was able to beat Jimmy Smith, the greatest male bowler of the early 1900s, in an outstanding exhibition match later recognized in "Ripley's Believe It or Not."

female bowlers of all time, are among the many standout performers who have spoken out against throwing the ball too hard.

"Excess speed is the No. 1 cause for not getting a strike on a pocket hit," Weber said. Like millions of other bowlers, Weber has been exasperated by watching a perfectly placed ball not produce a strike. What Weber and McCutcheon and others have learned is that too much speed will not permit the pins to mix well enough, sending one or more of them sailing too high or too wide or too quickly to take out other pins. An otherwise well-executed hook shot will lose much of its effectiveness because it will skid too far, not rolling long enough, and will "blow out" the pins instead of permitting them to mix the way they should. Bowlers who have stared disbelievingly at strange leaves after throwing the ball full force into the strike pocket have often concluded —sometimes rather reluctantly—that Weber and Mrs. McCutcheon and all those others are right. Much to their amazement and delight, those bowlers who have learned to curb their speed have found that their scores began to rise.

Most of today's bowlers are not familiar with Mrs. McCutcheon, the first prominent woman bowler in the world and one of the most respected bowling instructors in the history of the game. One of the first lessons Mrs. McCutcheon learned about bowling, and one she passed on to all her pupils, was that there was no virtue in flinging the ball mightily. Over and over, Mrs. Mac used the same words to impress this upon her students: "Let your ball roll. Don't try to throw it. Bowling means rolling." Mrs. Mac's advice is just as sound today as it was years ago.

HEAD AND EYES

From the moment you take your stance and all the way through the delivery, you should keep your eyes focused on your target. This requires concentration. There are times when bowlers who use spot or line aiming find that the temptation to sneak a look at the pins during the approach is too much to resist. They soon find out that such a peek, particularly if it involves a quick lifting of the head, is costly. Timing, aim and release can be thrown off by stealing a glance at the pins. The best way to avoid a sneak peek is to realize that it won't help you in any way. Indeed, it can only cause problems.

Without realizing it, some bowlers rock their head from side to side or bob it up and down during the approach. Either action can create havoc. From the start to the finish of the delivery, the head must be kept level. Concentration and eyes on target are the best ways to correct head movement.

THE RIGHT HAND AND WRIST

One of the secrets of bowling well is to keep movement to a minimum during the approach. Many bowlers aren't even aware they are guilty of jiggles and wiggles. This is especially true of little things done by the right hand and wrist, for they are often too subtle or quick or hidden to be detected.

"Cupping the ball" can be one problem. Cupping is rotating the wrist clockwise so that too much of the ball's weight is carried by the right hand. It seems innocent enough and it may feel comfortable, but those who do it are probably not aware that, in order to get their thumb back into the desired eleven-o'clock or handshake position during the pushaway, they will have to do some fancy work with their hand. It is so much easier to put the hand into the proper position right from the start and eliminate all the extra movement later. Some high-scoring bowlers find it natural to cup the ball. That's fine. But if you are not bowling well, part of the problem could be the cupping.

A more common fault, even among the pros, is to grip the ball too hard. Most bowlers squeeze the ball to some degree during their delivery, but too tight a grip restricts the swing and release, both of which should be rather effortless. It is almost impossible for anyone to observe any squeezing, so you alone will have to develop an awareness of how tightly you grasp the ball.

Keeping the wrist firm throughout the delivery is no easy chore. However, a wrist strap usually does a good job of locking the wrist in place. This emphasis on wrist control is not without purpose. Unless the wrist is firm throughout the approach, there will very likely be an inconsistency in the point of release and, in turn, the path of the ball down the lane. Anyone having wrist-control trouble is apt to have his or her shot drift to one side or the other. Then, in an attempt to correct, the bowler often overcompensates and the ball drifts the other way. All of this ruins accuracy and consistency with an obvious result: dwindling scores.

SHOULDERS

Years ago, "aim with your shoulders" used to be an oft-repeated aphorism. That expression is almost never uttered today. Amid the assortment of theories about how to bowl, the importance of the shoulders appears almost to have vanished. "Keep your shoulders squared to the pins" is the advice usually given today, and rightly so. Shoulders that are tilted to the right or to the left will cause shots that wander accordingly. Yes, it is true, as the old-timers liked to

A B   C

A straight, unhurried armswing will work wonders. If the ball is brought straight back past the right hip (A) and to its peak (B), it will be easier to start the ball on its forward path (C) toward the release point (D). All of this will lead to a

put it, that much of the aiming is done with the shoulders, but square shoulders are basic. It is also vital to keep the shoulders relaxed right from the taking of the stance through the placement of the ball. Bowlers who tighten up their shoulders tend to have difficulty getting a fluid armswing. One of the easiest and best ways to loosen the shoulders is to shrug or roll them a few times while still in your stance.

ARMSWING

If there is a shortcut to curing many of the problems that can be encountered during the approach, it is the use of the straight armswing from start to finish. Maintaining a straight arm is an easy way to zero in on your target. It cuts down on error, promotes shot accuracy and helps prevent problems such as forcing or pulling the ball.

That is saying an awful lot for the benefits of using an armswing that is arrow straight. But that, according to many high-average rollers, is no over-statement. One of the many fine bowlers who have felt that the armswing was the single most important facet of the game was the late Frank Clause, whose teaching methods worked wonders for more than a few of his pupils. Clause

D E

natural follow-through in which the arm will continue upward on its straight course (E).

was fond of saying, "The armswing should be like taking a train trip. If you come back with your arm by way of the Santa Fe, don't bring it forward by way of the Lackawanna. Come forward on the Santa Fe, too."

One of the bad habits easiest to pick up is bending the right arm on the downswing and bringing the ball behind the body. Deviating from the straight-line path almost always forces a compensation which, sadly, is usually insufficient to make up for the original error. Three things are bound to happen when the swing is not straight: (1) The ball will be brought back to the *left* of a straight line. (2) In trying to make up for that, the forward swing will have to be to the *right* of the desired path. (3) As the moment of release nears, the arm and the ball must be forced back to the *left,* causing the shot to take off in that direction. That's trouble.

Fortunately, correcting a faulty armswing is relatively uncomplicated. Time, patience and practice will straighten things out. The armswing should be a pendulumlike motion.

Let's review. The first thing on the downswing that both ball and arm do is to move freely past the right leg and hip. If your arm barely brushes against your hip or body, don't worry. That is usually all right and proof that you don't have a case of "flying elbow." Should the elbow slip off to the left during the downswing, you will have the dilemma described in the 1-2-3 scenario above.

Should the elbow fly off to the right, there will be a reversal of the situation with a resultant compensation to the left on the forward swing and then possibly back to the right at release.

Don't be discouraged if the trouble persists. Even the best of bowlers have had problems with their armswings. Eddie Lubanski, a member of the ABC Hall of Fame, and Jim Stefanich, one of the biggest winners on the Professional Bowlers Association circuit, were nagged by meandering armswings. Both Lubanski and Stefanich overcame the problem by using an age-old remedy: placing a folded towel under the right arm during practice sessions. If the towel dropped to the floor, they knew their arm had gone off to the right; if the towel stayed put, they knew they were overcoming their flyaway tendency. Stefanich even went beyond the towel routine and for a while had a piece of material strapped high up on his right side. When the inside of Jim's right arm rubbed against the material, he knew his swing was in line.

Don't apply any muscle to the swing; just let the weight of the ball carry it back and then straight ahead. Like a pendulum: tick-tock. After a pendulum swings back to a peak, it is carried in the opposite direction as its weight causes a shift in inertia. Of its own accord, your arm will straighten out to a full extension, with the elbow firmly locked at the bottom of the downswing and throughout the back-to-front swing—that is, your arm will straighten out provided you keep the swing free, natural, unhurried and unforced. Perhaps it sounds hard to execute like that. It isn't. Let the ball—not the hand or arm or elbow or muscles—do the work. It's safer that way. It's easier that way. With practice, you will get it down to clockwork.

FOOTWORK

The late Jimmy Smith, still considered one of the finest bowlers of all time, used to say over and over, "Footwork is the foundation of bowling." Smith knew what he was talking about. Legions of bowlers have learned that despite having excellent form in many areas—eyes fixed on the target area, head erect, wrist firm, shoulders loose and squared to the target, pendulum armswing—they were done in by shoddy footwork.

PBA Hall of Famer Don Johnson found from teaching bowling that men and women usually have distinct and opposite difficulties with their footwork. "Men generally get the ball into the swing too early and that causes them to hurry their footwork to catch up to the ball," Johnson pointed out. "With the women, it seems that 90 percent of them get the ball into their swing a little

A   B

Whether you finish your slide with the ball of your trailing foot flat on the floor (A), with your toes tucked under (B) or with some other form is largely a matter of developing a style that is comfortable for you. One thing is imperative, though: The sliding foot should be pointed directly down the lane.

late. Therefore, their footwork is very slow and they invariably end up ahead of the ball at the foul line."

Timing is something that bowlers do a lot of talking about, and sooner or later they come to realize that timing is governed by footwork. Hurrying feet can wreck an otherwise smooth delivery by causing a bowler to drop the ball behind the foul line, since the footwork will be ahead of the armswing. Dawdling feet can befoul matters just as badly. If the hand is ready to release the ball, and if the sliding foot is still a long way from the foul line, there will be an inclination to let go of the ball too soon. So the bowler will often try to slow down the rest of the body to wait for the sliding foot to catch up and may, as a result, wind up looking like a pretzel while twisting and straining at the foul line. Hesitating between any of the steps during the approach is an almost sure-fire way to botch up your timing. If you find that you come to a partial or complete stop during the approach, make every effort to get out of the habit before it becomes ingrained in your game.

THE SLIDE

Although the slide should be one of the easiest parts of the approach to master, many bowlers, especially novices, have trouble with it. Properly executed, the slide begins on the ball of the left foot at a point in line with or a little behind the right foot. A bending of the left knee is desirable; the deeper the bend, the

With a badly angled slide,
this lady is a splendid
candidate for a right-side
gutterball.

less you will have to lean forward from the waist. Bowlers who drag, rather than slide, their left foot often wind up stumbling along the foul line because their left foot has been kept flat and the rubber heel on their shoe has made contact too early with the floor, causing a rather abrupt slowdown. As with all other parts of the approach, the slide should be smooth and fluid.

Pay attention to the direction of the slide. Don't spoil an otherwise fine delivery by angling your slide off to one side or the other. And, when you are releasing the ball, don't suddenly point your toes to the left or to the right. The straighter the slide and the straighter the direction of the toes, the less risk you will have of running into trouble.

Bending at the Waist and Knee

How much you bend at the waist (lean forward) is largely dependent upon how much you bend your left knee during the slide to the foul line. If you are getting on in years or are heavy-set, it will probably be less demanding to do more bending at the waist than at the knee. Settling on the right combination ultimately comes down to doing whatever is comfortable and natural for you. The waist-knee bend should, however, bring your body down low enough so that the ball will land about two or three feet beyond the foul stripe. It's all right if the ball hits the lane somewhat closer, but if it lands much past the optimum point, it will take a bounce or two before it settles down. Lots of bowlers who don't get low enough try to make up for it by dropping their right shoulder. That merely compounds the problem. In addition to not bending sufficiently, they get their shoulders out of line and, as a result, their shot skitters off the side.

The bend of the left leg will be at its deepest point during the slide, for it will be supporting the weight of the body. At the same time, there should be lessening of the bend at the waist to compensate for the forward thrust of the left leg and the forward swing of the right arm.

For many bowlers, the key to having enough bend starts way back when they take their stance on the approach. What they do is immediately get into almost a sitting position, as if they were about to sit in a chair. Lowering the body this way, having the knees cracked a little and tilting forward slightly from the waist can be very comfortable. And many bowlers find that it makes for a smoother all-around delivery, since they acquire the proper bend with less effort and with less risk of upsetting their rhythm than by leaning forward or bending their knee too suddenly.

BALANCE

By now you may believe that coordinating all the facets of the approach is getting a bit complicated. Relax. Don't worry about getting it all down pat right from the start. It will take time.

Where does balance fit into all of this? Balance is that somewhat mystical element that brings everything together. Balance is a blending of the ingredients: stance, pushaway, shoulders, head, footwork, armswing—the whole ball of wax. A foulup of any one of these is often not that bad in itself. But if your footwork or pushaway or armswing is not executed correctly, there will usually

A   B

This sequence illustrates a progression of bad errors in a delivery. First, the bowler has started his backswing with the ball too far from his body (A). This results in the ball being wrapped way up behind his left hip at the height of the

be an attempt (conscious or otherwise) to compensate somewhere along the line. And, once you start to compensate for a fault in one area, you are almost surely going to mess up something else, which will require further compensation. There simply is not enough time during the approach to make up for a series of mistakes. Also, there is no need to get into this crisis situation in the first place. That's why you must build and blend all the subtleties of the approach one by one, making certain that there is not even one bugaboo that will throw the process out of synchronization.

There is probably no better way to spruce up your game than to work on balance. In order to keep your balance all the way through the approach, you

C   D

backswing (B). He then delivers with a badly angled slide and the ball too far away from his left foot (C). In an effort to correct, he pulls the ball violently with an across-the-body follow-through (D). All this can only lead to an erratic game.

will have to be doing a lot of things correctly. If you are having difficulties, try to think through each phase of your approach to find out where you are going wrong. Or have another bowler observe you and tell you where you are flubbing up.

Four of the most prominent reasons for getting out of balance are dropping the right shoulder, swinging the right arm on a curved path, not having enough bend in the left knee, and turning the sliding foot as you near the foul line.

If you lower the right shoulder, you will obviously force your body to that side, and to compensate for that, you will probably rush your feet so they can provide support. The solution is obvious: Don't drop your right shoulder. Try

This bowler's stance is fine—except that he is holding the ball too far to his right. This seems harmless enough, but he is apt to start his backswing at an angle, a good way to destroy the smooth, straight pendulum swing he should be trying to achieve.

walking through your approach again and again until you have learned to keep your shoulders squared. There is no better way of doing this than in front of a mirror.

Also, a roundhouse armswing will pull a bowler off balance. Those who have this problem are often unaware that they are bringing their right arm behind their body on the backswing and, to compensate, they are swinging the arm out to the right on the forward swing which, with the weight of a heavy ball, will pull the body off balance. That will inevitably lead to another compensation, usually whipping the right arm back to the left toward the end of the forward swing, a maneuver that will almost surely cause the ball to be released too much to the left.

Correcting such a convoluted armswing is more complicated than squaring the shoulders, but practice will do the job. What you have to do is to tuck in the right arm closer to the body. Start by holding the ball lined up just outside the hip while still in your stance. Then make certain that when you bring it through the backswing, you do not twist the arm behind your back. If you can avoid that, you are well on the way to having a straight armswing. As you bring the ball forward, be certain it is still going on a straight path. Bowlers who are able to maintain a straight backswing but who have an off-to-the-right forward swing usually wind up with this dilemma because they have trouble getting their arm and the ball past their right hip and leg. This often occurs because the armswing is ahead of the footwork. The solution is to make sure that the right foot is extended back far enough so that the right hip will be out of the way and the arm will be able to swing freely ahead.

Not enough knee bend will frequently be the main problem for those who have the above-mentioned difficulty with their armswing. Without sufficient bend in the knee, the trailing leg will often not be back far enough to clear the way for the arm. Furthermore, when not bent properly, the body is too erect and the bowler tends to loft the ball too much. Professional bowlers like to talk about how they "sit down into the shot," meaning they have had a knee bend deep enough to permit them to nestle the ball down on the lane rather than to plop it there. Again, a fine way of developing a satisfactory knee bend is to practice in front of a mirror or to go to the lanes and walk through the approach until you automatically get the knee positioned correctly.

Another thing pro bowlers talk about is "planting" their sliding foot. This foot is going to be carrying most or all of the weight of the body immediately before, during and after the release of the ball, so the foot must be firm—planted, as it were. It is best to wind up with the toes of the left foot pointing straight down the lane.

What do you do if your foot refuses to stay planted and wants to pull up its roots? First of all, check to find out if your armswing is ahead of your footwork and if you are releasing the ball too soon. A quick arm and early release will often cause you to rise up on your toes a bit, a form of compensation that tries to help the body catch up with the ball. Don't let go of the ball until it is lined up with, or a few inches in back of, the tip of the left shoe. Doing that should give the left foot time to plant itself like a sturdy oak.

There is much, much more to balance. Other important aspects include keeping the head down, thrusting the left arm out and back, not rushing through the approach and releasing the ball smoothly.

Making Repairs and Spares

Are your feet scurrying about like a disco dancer's? Are you yanking your arm across your body as if you were trying to grab the bowler on the next lane? Are you winding up like a pretzel at the foul line? Is your ball meandering down the lane, paying absolutely no attention to the direction you want it to take? Yes? O.K., it's obvious your game needs some repairs. Let's go to work.

QUICK FEET

There are two variations of this most common mistake: rushing the footwork to catch up with a hasty armswing, or just plain having greased-lightning feet. If your problem is of the first variety, it is far wiser to slow down the armswing than to hurry the footwork. An armswing that is too quick frequently results from a faulty pushaway. Be sure your pushaway coincides with your first step and doesn't precede it. An early pushaway will botch up the timing right from the outset. If the pushaway is coordinated and the armswing is still too fast, it means you are getting the ball into the downswing too hastily. To avoid that, try a slightly exaggerated pushaway, one in which the

Split spares are one of bowling's great challenges. None is easy, but knowing how the pins react will help you master them.

ball, instead of being nudged slightly forward in the prescribed manner, is thrust forward more. That will give your left foot a chance to get under way smoothly and will eliminate the tendency to rush the first step.

Should there be nothing wrong with the pushaway and you are still plagued by quick feet, you almost certainly are forcing your armswing, muscling the ball through the backswing. It is easy to do but an absolute no-no. For years, bowlers have advised, "Let the ball swing the arm. Don't let the arm swing the ball." The momentum of the ball as it drops into the downswing will be ample to give you a solid backswing, one that will require no muscling up on your part. Think about it. Picture it in your mind. This may be enough to eliminate the problem at once. But if the habit of forcing the ball is a long-standing one you may have more difficulty with it. Forcing, as we have learned, can come from gripping the ball too tightly, probably because you are tense. Or it can happen because the ball has not been properly fitted to you, giving the sensation that it will slip. To compensate, you may start applying finger pressure at some point in the delivery or begin getting the ball up high enough so it can be more easily controlled. The solutions are obvious: Relax, or get a ball that fits.

If you have fast feet, yet your armswing appears O.K., two other things could be causing the problem: (1) You could be tilting so far to the right that your right foot would suddenly rush forward to provide balance. (2) You could be leaning too far forward, again causing an instinctive rush of the third step to try to restore balance. To correct No. 1, make certain your shoulders are square to the target and that the right shoulder is not drooping. If your shoulders are not the problem, your left arm may be the culprit, so check and be sure to thrust it out to the left to help maintain proper balance. To correct No. 2, simply straighten up a little—or a lot—depending on how much adjustment is needed to keep you balanced.

Maybe you are just one of those bowlers with naturally fast feet. If so, you probably have been told again and again that the solution to the problem is to take a slow third step so that your armswing can catch up with your footwork. It is a common bit of advice that at first might sound highly effective. But logical? Let's consider.

What happens if you take two quick steps and then slow down to let your armswing catch up? You might answer, "Well, that takes away a lot of the momentum that has been generated during the first two steps." True. But that's not all there is to it. Having taken two fast steps and then a slow one, what are you supposed to do with the fourth step? Go back to a quick pace, or stick with the suddenly slowed movement? Generally speaking, neither works. It is far, far better to coordinate the timing right from the start rather than attempt to correct in midstream and develop a herky-jerky motion. Smooth out your approach into one flowing series of motions rather than slowing your footwork. Let your momentum build by making certain your feet do not leave the floor —shuffling instead of stepping out with them.

If you absolutely, positively can't slow down—and there are quite a few bowlers who are unable to do so—then go to the other extreme: Speed up your armswing right from the start with a more vigorous pushaway so it will be in time with your scurrying feet. Keeping your approach smooth and well timed is difficult at top speed, but it can be done.

Whatever you do, be sure that the ball is at the top of the backswing one step before your slide. If it's not, work on your timing. The dividends are worth it. With the ball at the height of the backswing at the end of your third step, you will experience one of the most satisfying pleasures of the game—the right arm moving fluidly forward and the left foot sliding smoothly ahead as you coordinate perfectly your shot, footwork and armswing.

DROPPING THE BALL TOO SOON

What is a bowler to do when sliding to the foul line while the ball is too far back for a correct release? There is no choice: The ball must be released and, in this situation, the ball will drop too soon, landing either in front of the foul line or just barely beyond it. This won't happen if the ball is at the top of the backswing at the end of the third step. If the ball arrives there at the right moment, you will be able to have it in front of you as you finish the slide. An early release can also be caused by lowering the right shoulder, by too heavy a ball or by a ball that fits improperly.

LOFTING THE BALL

A ball that sails well past the foul line before crashing to the lane is not only a noisemaker, it is also a shot spoiler. Causes: thumb or finger holes that are too tight, body too erect at the finish, rushing your forward armswing to catch up with your feet, or getting your armswing ahead of your feet and then trying to hold back the release while the left foot slides. Remedies: Check your ball and grip, bend your left leg and/or lean forward more and improve your timing.

Teetering at the foul line is a sure sign of a poor delivery. Are you rushing? Angling your slide? Not maintaining balance with good arm and leg extension?

TEETERING AT THE FOUL LINE

Bowlers occasionally tightrope or stumble as they frantically try to avoid crossing the foul stripe. When that routine becomes commonplace, it is time to figure out what is wrong. Could it be that you are not extending your left arm and right leg to keep you in balance? Could it be you are glancing down at the foul line when your eyes should be focused on a target? Maybe you are angling your sliding foot too much or rushing so much that you cannot control your body.

HOOKING THE BALL TO THE BROOKLYN SIDE

If your hand and arm are across your body, instead of being extended toward the pins after the release, your shot is likely to slam into the left side of the headpin rather than the right side. Such a misdirected shot is called going to the Brooklyn side. To get rid of that habit, keep your right arm close to your side and be certain your fingers are coming out of the ball from the side, not from the top. Bowlers sometimes pull their shots because they drift to the right during their approach and then compensate by yanking their arm to the left. Keep the arm in tight, the fingers to the side and the approach straight. Goodbye, Brooklyn.

DRIFTING SHOTS TO THE RIGHT

One of the most exasperating of all experiences is when shot after shot after shot drifts to the right, missing or barely nipping the headpin. Experienced bowlers usually can diagnose what they are doing wrong. Novices often can't. They might not be aware their footwork is drifting off to the right. Or they may not realize they are not applying enough finger lift to the ball upon release. Or—and newcomers are especially prone to this—they may not detect that they are swinging their arm to the right rather than straight ahead. This usually happens when the ball is brought to the left and behind the body during the backswing, a twisting motion that generally forces the arm and ball to the right to get around the hip on the forward swing. When the swing is straightened out, the shot will be, too.

If this bowler knew what was going on in his backswing, he would realize that whipping the ball all the way behind his left hip destroys a smooth delivery. Result: frustration and low scores.

ADJUSTMENTS: THE MAGIC ELIXIR?

Let's be honest: there is no wondrous ingredient that will enable anyone to roll a string of 300 games or average 275 for a season. There is, however, a way of improving your scores that we haven't covered: making adjustments in your line of delivery. Theories and systems abound on how these adjustments should be executed.

The time for adjustments is when you are rolling the ball over your target but not hitting the strike pocket. To find out which method is most suitable for you, do some experimenting. In most cases this will involve shifting your stance more to one side or the other, or moving your target slightly. Make gradual changes until you achieve success, keeping in mind that it is generally true that each board you move your stance in one direction will generally result in a three-board shift in the opposite direction when the ball strikes the pins. If these adjustments don't work, try turning your shoulders a bit. For shots that are sailing to the left, angle your shoulders to the right throughout your delivery and vice versa.

Because of variations in temperature and humidity, lane conditions can change quickly, and this can dramatically affect your game. As a day's bowling wears on, lanes will also usually tend to cause more hook. Lane conditions are also affected by the type and amount of dressing applied: You often find a significant variation from one bowling center to another. There is even variation from one lane to another within the same house. Because of all this, you have to be able to adjust your shot. If the lanes are hooking excessively, it is often best to move your starting position a little to the left. When the lanes are tight, the adjustment should be to the right. Only by experimenting will you be able to make the adjustments most suitable for your shot.

FOR LEFT-HANDERS ONLY

"Give me a break!" has been the cry of many a bowler. In some ways, left-handers get breaks. But only if those lefties know how to exploit these advantages will they be able to benefit from them. Since there are relatively few left-handers, they seldom have to contend with the track that becomes worn into the right side of the lane by right-handers. After many shots have been rolled over the same area, the conditioning substance on the lane surface breaks down and a track is created. Although barely visible, this groove can bedevil bowlers by interfering with a line they would prefer to roll or by making them try to avoid the track by changing to a different angle.

The left side of the lane, however, is almost always track-free. So a left-hander can move to the outside, where shots can be fired into the pocket at more of an angle, since there won't be any worry that the ball will be nudged slightly off course when it crosses a track, which is usually around the second arrow. Being able to send the ball over the first arrow rather than over the second means that the ball will be able to enter the 1-2 left-handers' pocket at a sharper angle than right-handers are usually able to get. If a right-hander shoots over the first arrow, the ball would have to cross over the grooved second-arrow path to get into the 1-3 pocket. When a track gets deep, a right-hander may be forced to shoot over the third arrow, a move that allows little room for the ball to hook into the pocket.

The advantage to a lefty in being able to get more angle is that there will be less deflection of a hook ball when it tangles with the pins. Left-handers new to the game may be a trifle frightened about shooting over the first arrow, feeling that this puts the ball perilously close to the gutter, but it is a shot well

Earl Anthony is known for his very
smooth left-handed delivery . . .
and his consistently high scores.

worth working on, one that will not seem nearly so dangerous after a few strikes have been rolled. More of a worry than the proximity of the gutter is the tendency to pull the hand across the body, something left-handers often do when aiming for the first arrow. By keeping the elbow in tight and by using a straight armswing, the pulling will be ended.

STRIKE IT RICH WITH SPARES

The quest for strikes can become so intense that bowlers can forget the value of spares. To put things into perspective, consider what Mrs. Floretta McCutcheon, one of the all-time great women bowlers, had to say about spares: "My first impression was that the way to bowl was to throw as hard as possible. I stood as far back as I could and ran to the foul line. I often wonder why I didn't break my neck. Then, during my first league season, an elderly gentleman told me to concentrate on hitting the one-three pocket and to be more concerned about picking up spares than strikes. That became the foundation of my game. I wasn't afraid anymore of not getting strikes. In later years, people talked about my consistency at hitting the pocket. I think my accuracy was because of what that old man told me."

There is no such thing as an easy spare. Ask any bowler who has failed to convert the 1-5, the 9-10 or a single-pin leave. In all, there are 1,023 possible spare leaves. A lack of concentration is often the reason for failing to pick up allegedly easy leaves. Harder spares are frequently not converted for another reason: a lack of know-how. Harnessing your concentration is up to you. Acquiring know-how is something we will try to help you with.

From the back of the approach, it looks as if the pins in some close-together leaves are almost belly to belly. Actually, there is a distance of 12 inches from the center of one pin to the center of its neighbor or neighbors—the pin or pins that are closest to each other when there is no split. More important, the distance from the outer edge of the belly of one pin to the same spot on a neighboring pin is 7.2344 inches. The diameter of a ball is 8.5943 inches. Thus a ball cannot fit between two neighboring pins such as the 7-8 or the 4-5. To convert any of these "fit splits" the objective is to try to roll the ball between the pins. Since the ball can't fit in between them, down they go.

Unfortunately, not all spare leaves are as inviting as the fit splits. On difficult spare leaves, find a strike pocket where you want the ball to go. On the "bucket" leave, for example, where the 2-4-5 and 8 pins remain, consider the 2-5 as the strike pocket. If the ball hits in there properly, the 2 pin will fly to the left to wipe out the 4, and the 5 will veer off to topple the 8.

Select a key pin. The key pin should be the back pin in any double-wood leave such as the 1-5, the 2-8 or the 3-9. The key pin is so important since it is the one most likely to be left upright if you don't pick up the spare. Some splits—the 4-6, the 7-10 and the 4-6-7-10 among them—are almost impossible to convert. Turning splits such as these into spares is spectacular; missing them can be costly. To pull off a spare in such cases requires a perfect shot. You can easily miss all the pins, resulting in no further pinfall being added to your score. Unless making a difficult split is needed to win a match, it is much better to play it safe by trying to knock down the pin or pins that are easiest to get to.

Spare Shooting

When shooting for spares, always use as much of the lane as possible.

Right-Side Spares

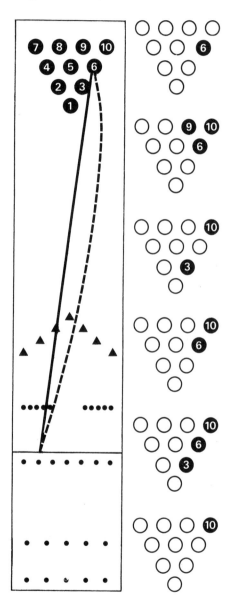

For right-side spares, take your stance well to the left of normal and try to angle the ball across the inside edge of the middle arrow.

Left-Side Spares

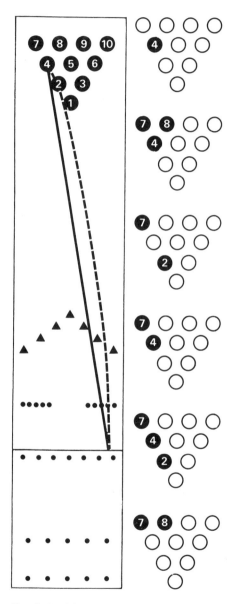

For left-side spares, move to the right of your usual spot.

Strike-Ball Spares

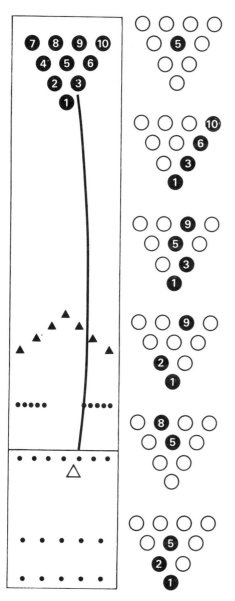

Middle Spares

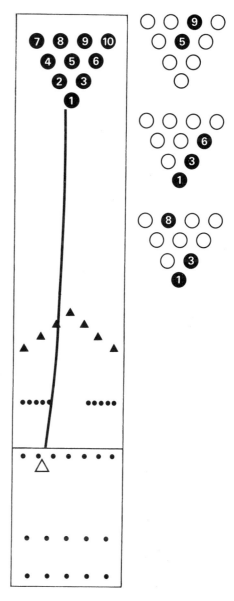

Strike-ball spares are so named because they can be picked up by rolling the ball as if there were a full rack of pins; balls that enter the 1–3 pocket will take care of any leftover pins.

Middle spares are best picked up by taking a stance just a bit to the left of your regular starting point and rolling the ball over the outer edge of the third arrow.

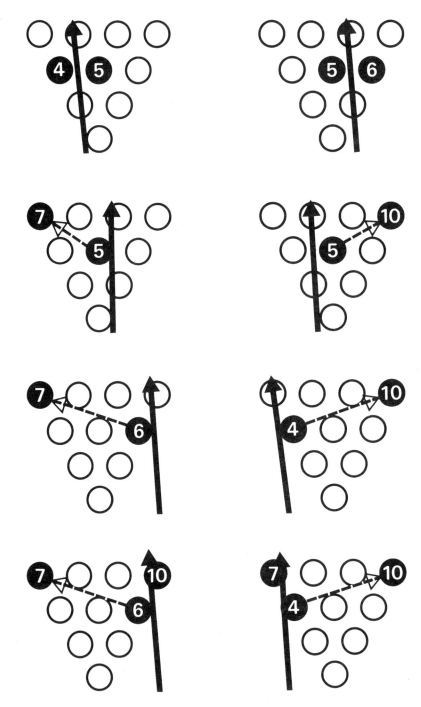

On split spares, accuracy is all important since you have to hit a key pin with enough precision so that it will deflect toward the other remaining pin or pins.

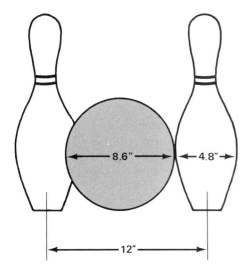

It is helpful to understand that the width of a bowling ball (8.59 inches) is greater than the gap between the midsections of any two adjacent pins (7.23 inches). This means that on "fit splits" the objective is to roll the ball between both pins. Because the ball cannot fit between the pins, it will hit the inside edges of both and knock them down.

Any formula for effective sparemaking centers on two prerequisites: keeping your body squared to the target and finding the best angle for the shot. The best angle involves using as much of the lane as possible by moving in the direction opposite of the leave. There are two angles: For the 7 pin and left-side spares, a right-hander moves to the extreme right; for the 10 pin and right-side spares, the shift is to the left. Also keep in mind the widely held rule that a one-board move on the approach will generally result in a three-board difference at the finish.

Do It Your Way

In the preceding chapters, there has been a lot of emphasis on precisely how to execute every phase of your delivery. Now we'd like to offer one overriding bit of advice: You will be better off if you bowl your own way. That's right, use your own style. Then why have we devoted so much space to an explanation of every little detail? Well, all the expertise *does* have a purpose. It gives a summation of the best overall techniques of bowling. But not all people are the same. Some are short, some are tall, others are skinny, many are heavy. Each has distinctive qualities; some of these will help, others will hinder his or her development as a bowler. That's why we say that you are going to be better off if you bowl your own way. We also say, with equal conviction, that you *must* learn to incorporate into your style as many of this book's basics as you can.

Rare is the bowler who can build a sound game and roll consistently high scores without having mastered at least the majority of the fundamentals. But you will probably find that some of our instruction will not blend with your style very well. That's fine. Adapt, alter, refine these tips and come up with ways that suit you best. Participants in all sports have a variety of styles, and bowlers

Don Carter, voted the greatest bowler of all time in a poll of sportswriters in the 1970s, had one of the shortest backswings of the game's stars.

are no different. Besides, tinkering with your game to build it to your own specifications is one of the most satisfying aspects of the sport. So sift through the tips, learn them and build your game around them.

There are and always have been high-scoring bowlers with unorthodox styles. The important thing about the variations in their styles is that they very likely are responsible for making those bowlers so successful. Had those bowlers strained to overcome their novel ways, they probably would not have been nearly as proficient. To reinforce the importance of building your game around your own natural style, here are examples of more than a dozen bowlers, almost every one of them a member of the ABC, WIBC or PBA Halls of Fame. Each had a peculiarity of style that became his or her trademark.

Among his idiosyncrasies on the lanes, Don Carter had almost no backswing with the ball. Neither did Billy Hardwick. That might have been one of the secrets of their success, but a similar style would probably have ruined Joe

Lou Campi's first association with a bowling game was in Italy where he learned boccie, a game where the bowler ends his approach on the right foot. He used the "wrong foot" approach to gain national acclaim, including winning the first PBA tournament title in 1959.

Falcaro, whose backswing was so high at its peak that it was almost straight over his head. Buddy Bomar never really heeded the adage about walking a straight line during the approach and, wiggling his way to the foul line, he rolled so many over-200 scores that he seemed to be a machine. Harry Smith went up to the line in an unusual way, hopping along like Bugs Bunny. Junie McMahon was one of several outstanding performers who had a swing like a figure eight.

Don Johnson, who won at least one major tournament each year from 1966 through 1977, was a man of great body english when bowling (above). One of the great bowling pictures (below) was taken as he fell to the floor after getting 11 strikes in a row—only to fail to get the twelfth strike for a 300 game and a special $10,000 prize in the 1970 Firestone Tournament of Champions.

The four-step approach to the foul line is almost universally taught by bowling instructors. That didn't keep Count Gengler from using only one step, or Adolph Carlson from taking two steps, or Lee Jouglard from employing a three-step approach, or Stan Gifford from using half a dozen or more steps. When it came to footwork, though, the style of Lou Campi was the most unusual. A right-hander, Campi violated the one seemingly inviolable rule of footwork by sliding to the foul line with his right foot. That was the way Campi had rolled the ball when he played boccie, a bowling-type game, back in his native Italy, and he saw no reason to alter his form for tenpins.

Charlotte Grubic had two idiosyncrasies on the lanes. She used to have such an explosive and high backswing that it seemed she fully intended to toss the ball behind her rather than down the lane. She also appeared to see a red light during her approach, coming to a stop between her first and second steps. Elvira Toepfer didn't stop until she had released the ball, but then she added her own brand of follow-through by kicking her right foot so high that it almost appeared she was trying to boot a field goal.

Hank Lauman used to veer off to the right during his approach. Jouglard, in addition to his three-step technique, used to crank up his throwing arm by taking a windmill swing before starting his steps. Steve Nagy, famous for lofting his shot well out onto the lane, was occasionally kidded about getting a strike on the first bounce. Carmen Salvino, a bowling sensation while just a teen-ager during the early 1950s, completely altered his game in the 1970s when his big curve ball lost its effectiveness because of the changing lane conditions. Radically restructuring his style with the help of his friend Hank Lahr, a nuclear physicist, the one-time big winner began winning again. When asked to explain how he had been able to become a champion again during his forties, Salvino said, "Now I bowl according to a mathematical equation." Although Salvino refuses to divulge the secret of that equation, one dramatic change is that he now lets the ball hang straight down at his side during his stance rather than holding it waist-high or higher, the way he had done for years.

Seeing a bowler here and another there who has an unusual style is one thing; but when an entire five-man team at the ABC Tournament all stooped over so far during their approach that it seemed they were trying the old push-the-peanut-with-your-nose routine, well, that was something else. When asked about the odd posture, the captain of the squad explained, "Our style may seem funny to others, but it was forced on us and it's hard to change. We come from a small town where we have only one bowling center. It's a basement layout of six lanes. The ceiling is low and there are pipes above the approaches. You learn to stay low and to duck—or you bust your head."

Mark Roth, a dominant figure on the PBA tour, uses a pronounced wrist cock at the top of his backswing.

The two most dominant performers on the PBA circuit during the 1970s —left-hander Earl Anthony and right-hander Mark Roth—are both adamant that unorthodox tactics have been instrumental in their record-setting performances.

"My bent elbow plays an important part in my ability to control the speed of my shots," Anthony begins. "That's why the bent elbow is deliberate. I can control the ball better in the backswing and can adjust my speed. It also gives me more accuracy because I have a tendency to push the ball on the lane rather than to throw it." Using his bent-elbow delivery, Anthony in 1975 became the first bowler ever to earn $100,000 during a single PBA season.

Roth's form is radically different from that of most professionals. He has an excessively high backswing, at the top of which he cocks his wrist. And, with a series of as many as eight quick stutter steps, Roth races to the foul line, whips his arm forward and gives the ball a tremendous counterclockwise turn on release. His style is more violent than smooth, more awkward than elegant. But Roth knows what he is up to. This is what he has to say about his own game —and yours:

"I tried going to a four-step delivery, which is what most top players recommend. But I felt off-balance. I also lost something off the ball. I threw it slower . . . and lost some of my accuracy. I felt I was forcing the ball. It didn't take me long to go back to my normal six-step style. With six steps, I can keep my arm in really tight and generate more power.

"The best advice I can give to any bowler is this: Stick to your own style and don't copy anybody. Each individual should bowl with the style that's natural. So stick with the basics and incorporate them into your game; you will have a better chance to reach your true potential."

However you roll the ball, one of the pleasures of bowling is the joy of a good hit.

10

Practice: The Key to a Successful Game

Practice. It can be drudgery. It can be wearying. It can also be exhilarating, enjoyable, challenging and rewarding.

Listen to what Earl Anthony, one of bowling's greats, has to say about working at the game: "What I've done to get where I am isn't really a secret," he says. "What it amounts to is a lot of hard work. . . . Before I came on the tour, I put in seven days of practice a week, every week, for four years. And I'd throw shadow balls [shots taken when the pins have been removed from the lane] four to six hours a day. You talk about boring; *that's* boring. But it was something I felt was necessary because it's the kind of dedication and hard work it takes to be successful on the tour."

Far out? Definitely. But there is no need for you to push yourself that hard unless you aspire to a career as a professional bowler. Set your own pace. Practice once or twice a week, or once or twice a month, or once or twice a year. That might not sound like much help if you are wondering "How often shall I be practicing?" And yet the answer depends on how skilled a bowler you want to become. Whatever your objective—to become the finest bowler in your school, on your team, in your neighborhood, in your town, in your coun-

109

try, for that matter—any realistic hope that it will come true will depend largely upon how often, how diligently and how wisely you practice. So practice as often as possible, daily if you have serious ambitions.

HOW TO PRACTICE

Just spending a lot of time practicing will not automatically transform a low-average bowler into a high-average one. To get the maximum benefit from those extra hours at the lanes, there must be a specific purpose to them. *How* you practice will be of far greater importance than *how long* you practice. How you practice is something that should be planned. The best way to approach this is to jot down the facets of your game that need some doctoring. Knowing what is wrong is only half of what should be written down. The other half—how to overcome those ills—will determine exactly what you will be working on at practice time. If the list of repairs runs on for page after page, that is all right, for it will indicate an awareness of your problems and be the first step toward solving them. It is when you have absolutely no idea of what you are doing wrong that you are *really* in hot water. But even then, all is not lost. Ask the resident pro or another good bowler to watch you roll for a while so he or she can help determine where you are slipping up. While you are at it, ask for some tips on how to correct what you are doing wrong. Pros are usually paid for such help, so keep that in mind.

If your weaknesses are as long as the family shopping list, pick out the one you feel is most important to zero in on and then devote your entire practice period to overcoming it. One session might not do it. But persistence is bound to pay off.

There is no such thing as a slump that can't be broken or a mistake that can't be remedied. Put your brains, and those of others, to work, and though you might not work miracles you will make steady progress.

Some of the following recommendations are, admittedly, offbeat. All, however, have been used successfully. Pick out the ones that appeal to you most and try them first. Then, even if a few of the others don't capture your fancy, give them a try. You may well be pleasantly surprised by how effective they can be.

Dispensing with scorekeeping has been of considerable help to some bowlers. Jotting down strikes, spares, splits and the like can be distracting and subtly cause a bowler to get away from the primary purpose of the workout without even being aware of it. Your attention can shift from solidifying your game to seeing if you can achieve a certain score. And, with the pins on the deck, and the scoresheet at the ready, many bowlers tense up even though it is only practice. As one instructor put it, "In practice, a bowler often will be too embarrassed to continue if his or her scores are much below their normal. They sometimes suspect that somebody may be secretly laughing at their ineptness." Scrap that notion. You are entitled to use any methods you want during practice. That's your time to experiment, change, correct, try new things. The only person you have to be concerned with is yourself.

Forget about pinfall during practice. How? There are three dandy ways: (1) Simply do not keep score. (2) Don't even bother using pins. (3) Don't roll a single ball. Should you wish to avoid the distraction of the pins, just tell someone at the control and the request will be accommodated.

Bowlers sometimes merely walk through their entire approach without a ball, as they try to get their timing synchronized. Obviously, there is a difference between just walking your approach without a ball and going through it while swinging one. So once you have things in working order, pick up a ball and see if your timing holds up. If it doesn't, try to find the problem. Since your sole goal here is to straighten out your timing, work without pins and don't even watch where or how the ball rolls. When your timing is off, your game will become riddled with errors that creep in as you try to compensate in one way or another. As soon as you get your timing down pat, you can go on to other things. A word of caution: Don't be satisfied that your timing is in order just because it has clicked well on two or three tries; once you get it synchronized, keep repeating it until you are sure it will not desert you on your next trip to the lanes.

Let's say that you have come to the lanes with all good intentions of improving your timing but that no amount of trying works. That is not at all uncommon. You probably have lost your "feel." Feel is something you develop even if you have been bowling only a short time. Then, when you try new techniques, it is only natural that you will feel awkward for a while. This is true whether you are working on timing, a new release, an in-tight armswing or anything else. To be prepared for this, remind yourself that there will be a period when you will feel uncomfortable, but that as long as you are doing things properly, this will be replaced by a new feeling of comfort, one predicated on the knowledge that you are doing things as they should be done.

PICKING LANES

Give some thought to what lanes you practice on. It's a good idea to use the same pair of lanes for most of your workouts. After you have rolled on them a number of times, you will know them well enough so they can aid you in detecting mistakes in your game. It is helpful, for example, for you to *know* that lane No. 22 is ideal for your late-breaking hook shot. Game after game, your ball snaps off at just the right instant. If, suddenly, your ball begins breaking far too early and hits the No. 1 pin too flush, you can be quite certain that this problem has not been brought about by the lane, for you know good ol' No. 22 far too well. Knowing what is going wrong brings up the other half of the dilemma: *Why* is your shot hooking too soon? Think about the possible reasons and, on your next few shots, try to figure out what you are doing differently. It may be that you are turning the ball too much at release and making it behave more like a curve than a hook. Or it may be that you decreased your arm speed, or that you are finishing too far behind the foul line, or that you are releasing the ball a little too much to the left. Carefully work through to the solution.

Many bowlers waste much of their practice time because they are watchers rather than observers. Yes, there *is* a difference—an important one. Merely watching the ball and the pins means that you are not *thinking* about what you are seeing. Old-timer Frank Clause put it this way: "You've got to think, think, THINK. You're not a machine. You can go through approximately the same motions time after time, but you can't go through them exactly the same way. One day you're tired, the next day you're fresh and alert. Sometimes you don't feel well and a bowling ball seems to weigh a ton. At other times it feels like a feather and you throw it with too much speed. You've got to react—and fast —not only to lane conditions but also to your own physical condition. Most important, don't get panicky and don't press when things go wrong. Figure out what the trouble is and do something about it."

Can such thinking really pay off? Let's have Dick Weber answer that. "I once rolled a series of 245, 161, 267," Weber recalls. "I couldn't do anything right in that second game. My timing was off. My feet and arms weren't coordinated. My ball kept diving into the headpin at the last moment, and when I moved to the left, I didn't have enough stuff on the ball to carry the pins.

Luckily I pulled out of it in time to finish with a good game. What did I do? Well, I thought about things and realized I was more tired than I felt. I just wasn't getting the speed I needed. So I held the ball higher than I usually do at the start of my approach, gave it a bigger pushaway and my speed came back."

Practicing on the same pair of lanes has its values. There are, however, benefits to using other lanes. Switching around will give you a chance to study how your ball reacts with varying lane conditions and, what really counts, will present an opportunity for you to experiment to find the best methods for those conditions. There are so many variables from one lane to another and there are so many adjustments that can be made that it is almost impossible to keep all the details in mind. The best thing to do is to write down some notes about how to cope with these situations.

KEEPING A NOTEBOOK

You might want to keep a notebook filled with tips and reminders, for this distillation of information can come in handy when you want to refresh your memory. When Denny Turner of Stockton, California, joined the PBA tour in 1974, he armed himself with a green three-ring notebook. Some of his notations read: "Eye on target. Tell yourself after each shot where the ball crossed the arrows." Also in his notebook were these six "musts": "(1) foot on spot; (2) thumb at nine o'clock; (3) eye on target, not pocket; (4) pushaway; (5) don't get uptight; bowl your best each shot; relax and enjoy; (6) while bowling, always think about your bowling, nothing else."

A notebook is a handy way to keep track of tips and reminders about your game.

DEVELOPING A RELAXED GRIP

Once you have advanced beyond the rudiments of bowling, spend some time developing your feel and instincts. One of the most vital aspects of feel centers on gripping the ball correctly. And the most important part of this is to have a grip that is relaxed. Squeezing the ball with the fingers will reduce your sensitivity or feel for the ball and give you sore fingers. So relax and grip the ball gently. You will have a better feel for the ball all the way through the approach, which will make for a smoother release. If your grip is too tight, work on easing it. Let the ball dangle at your side for a while without applying any pressure from your fingers. Then carefully move into the pushaway and start your approach, concentrating on staying relaxed. The ball and you should work as one. If, perchance, the ball slips out of your grasp when dangling it, check with the pro shop to be sure the ball has been drilled properly for you.

DEVELOPING FEEL

Feel is a process of becoming so completely familiar with your form that you will be able to detect even the most minute deviations from your normal pattern. This requires many, many hours on the lanes, hours that will pay off when you reach the level where, with little or no thought, you will realize that a kink has cropped up in your swing. This sort of feel might be classified as instinct, although that term is usually reserved for the hairline adjustments that not too many bowlers are capable of making. The simplest way of distinguishing between feel and instinct is this: If you can tell when you have finished a shot that you have done something differently, that is feel; if you can sense that you are doing something different or wrong before rolling the ball and are able to correct matters before it's too late, that is instinct.

Although instinct more often than not is something that a person naturally has or does not have, it can be acquired or sharpened to some extent. This requires knowing your game inside, outside and upside down. It also requires knowing what to do and how to do it when the time comes to make tiny last-second changes. Instinct can be a marvelous asset.

One final observation about practice: Get away from it now and then if you feel you are not benefiting from it. Staying away from the lanes for a while might be just the tonic that is needed. After such a break, you may find that your interest in the game has been renewed and that you are able to grasp parts of it that had eluded you in the past. One of the nicest things about practice is that it enables you to gain confidence in your game and in yourself when you are able to repair matters. Practice has its rewards, so make it a part of your routine.

Keeping score is part of the fun of the game. Score-projection units help bowlers keep track of who is doing what by projecting scores on overhead screens.
When the game is over the scorekeepers dutifully double-check all the figures.

11

Keeping Score

Today's system of scoring was instituted way back in September 1895 at Beethoven Hall in New York City when the ABC was founded. At that meeting, a Louis Stein spoke up loud and long in favor of the 300 scoring system and finally convinced enough of the delegates present to adopt it. Before that, there had been all sorts of scoring rules, the most prevalent of which permitted a maximum score of 200. The vote on which system to use was extremely close, but Stein's proposal carried because he was able to convince others that a score of 300 would be the most appealing to bowlers since it allowed more room for improvement.

THE 300-POINT SYSTEM

X/ – OF. That is the bowling "alphabet." The only other markings on a scoresheet are numerical ones showing frame-by-frame scoring and the final score. There are ten frames in a game, with each frame consisting of one or two shots except for the tenth, in which it is possible to roll a maximum of three balls. A one-shot frame occurs when the bowler rolls a strike. To designate a strike, an "X" is placed in the left of the two smaller boxes at the top of each frame. This double-box scoring system was devised to cut down on scoring errors and to make it easy to audit and correct scores. It is required by both WIBC and ABC rules.

If a strike is not made, the number of pins that have been knocked down with the first shot is marked in the upper left box. A small circle (O) is used to signify a split and is drawn around the pinfall number in the left-hand box. The bowler gets a second shot in any frame in which a strike is not recorded. If all the remaining pins are toppled with that second shot, that constitutes a spare and is noted in the upper right box with a diagonal slash (/). When anything less than a spare is attained, the number of pins felled with shot No. 2 is placed in the upper right box. A dash (–) is put in the second box to indicate an error, meaning that the bowler has either missed a single-pin leave or has failed to pick up any of the pins that were left standing.

"F" is for foul, which is assessed when any part of a player contacts the lane or any structure beyond the foul line. It is perfectly legal, though, for the hand or the arm to extend over the foul line during a normal follow-through. A foul negates any pins that were knocked down with that shot and results in no score for that roll.

ADDING IT ALL UP

The only complicated part of keeping score stems from the unique cumulative-scoring process of the game, which makes it possible to have a score as high as 30 in a box. This comes from the reward given for rolling a strike. When a strike is rolled, the score for that frame is not complete until the results of the next two shots are added to it.

Let's assume that JoAnn rolls a strike in the fourth frame. That is worth 10 pins. If JoAnn rolls similar deck-clearing shots on her subsequent two shots, her total pinfall for the fourth frame would be 30. Those 30 pins would then be added to her score through the third frame and the total would be marked in the fourth-frame box.

A spare entitles the bowler to add the pinfall from the next shot to the score for that frame. Only in one frame, the tenth, can as many as three shots be taken. That comes about only when a bowler is able to roll a strike on the first ball of that frame or a spare on the first two shots. It is possible to roll as many as twenty-one balls in a game (spares in each of the first nine frames and then three shots in the tenth) or as few as twelve. The rationale behind allowing bowlers to toss as many as three balls in the final frame is that it presents the possibility of rolling a perfect game—a nice round 300 based on twelve consecutive strikes that would result in a maximum of 30 pins in each of the ten frames.

A SAMPLE GAME

To check your understanding of scoring, let's run through a hypothetical game by someone named Joshua.

JOSHUA	7 –	⑦ /	9 /	5 4	9 /	F /	☒	8 /	☒	☒ ☒ 9	
	7	15	30	39	49	69	89	109	139	168	168

Frame 1—On his first shot, Joshua knocks down 7 pins, a total that is jotted down in the small left-hand box. Shot No. 2 misses the 3 upright pins, so place a dash (–) in the small box on the right and credit Joshua with a score of 7 for that frame.

Frame 2—Once again, Joshua topples 7 pins with his first shot. This time, however, they are not bunched. To indicate that he has left a gaping split (in this case 4-7-10), circle the 7 that is placed in the left box. The second shot takes care of only the 4 pin. This is recorded by putting a 1 in the right box. Joshua's score of 8 for that frame is then added to that of the preceding frame, and the total of 15 is marked at the bottom of the box.

Frame 3—A 10-pin tap. Joshua's first shot does everything but get rid of that stubborn 10 pin. Credit him with a 9 in the left box and then place a horizontal slash (/) in the right box after he wipes out the 10 pin with his second shot. Don't put any score at the bottom of the box, though, Josh, because of his spare, gets to add the pinfall from one more shot to that total.

Frame 4—Joshua's ball hooks too soon, hits the headpin almost on the nose and brings down only 5 pins. Adding those 5 to the previous frame's spare gives him a total of 15 pins in the third. That 15, plus the score of 15 for the first two frames, results in a total of 30, which is marked at the bottom of the box for frame No. 3. On his second shot, Joshua spills 4 pins. That gives him a 9 for the frame and a total of 39 for the first four frames.

49

69

89

109

139

168

Frame 5—This time the 10 pin goes down. But the 7 stays up. Altogether, Joshua topples 9 pins on his first shot. He then disposes of the 7 pin with his second roll. So give him credit for a spare. Hold off on marking down the overall score, though. That spare means Josh adds the result of the next shot to the fifth-frame total.

Frame 6—A strike. Wait a minute. Joshua stumbled across the foul line, and his foot wound up on the lane. Foul. Jot down an "F" in the left-hand box. And, since Josh cannot be awarded any extra pins for the fifth frame, conclude his scoring there by adding the 10 for his spare to the previous 39. His total score now is 49. Undismayed, Joshua fells all 10 pins with his next shot. That's not a strike, however, because it was his second ball of the frame. But it is a spare.

Frame 7—At long last, Josh rolls a strike that is truly a strike. "X" marks the strike in the left-hand box. And the 10 pins fill out his score for frame No. 6, giving him a 20 there and an overall 69.

Frame 8—It would have been nice to get a double, but an 8 on the first ball and a 2 on the second result in a spare. Place an 8 in the left box, a slash (/) in the right box. And, since the strike of the previous frame means the next two shots are added there, credit Joshua with 20 pins in Frame No. 7, raising his score to 89.

Frame 9—A strike. That's worth an "X" in the ninth frame, an extra 10 pins in the eighth and a score through that point of 109.

Frame 10—Zeroed in, Joshua tosses two strikes in a row and finishes up with a 9 on his last ball. These two strikes round out the scoring for the ninth frame and give him 139. For the tenth frame, Josh had a score of 29 (X-X-9), bringing his final score to 168.

12

Bowling Etiquette

Envision a forty-lane bowling establishment with two five-player teams on each pair. That's two hundred bowlers. It also adds up to wall-to-wall noise. But, thanks to the bowlers themselves, all this hustle and clattering does not disintegrate into mass confusion. The reason order prevails is because most bowlers adhere to well-established rules of conduct and play, rules based on common sense and a respect for the rights of others. They can be broken down into two categories: rules of courtesy and traffic rules.

RULES OF COURTESY

First of all, show up at the lanes in plenty of time to roll when your team is scheduled to begin competition. Your teammates are counting on you. If you are late, it can be upsetting to them and could affect their chances of winning. Once at the lanes, make sure that you are ready to bowl when your turn comes. Each team has a lineup, so everyone knows when his or her turn is coming up and should prepare accordingly.

If you notice that someone is using a towel or rosin or powder that you forgot to bring along, don't help yourself to it without first asking permission. Bowlers are generally a congenial lot and usually will be willing to share. Just ask before you use.

Once you have begun bowling, you may find that the approach is not exactly the way you would like it to be. Thus you might be tempted to apply some powder or chalk or rosin to the approach to make it stickier or easier to slide on. That might suit your needs, but it also might create havoc for other bowlers. If you feel the approach needs some fixing up, don't hesitate to report this to the control desk or the manager of the lanes.

Many bowlers like to have some refreshments while competing. That's fine. Usually there are tables or holders in the seating area where food and beverages can be placed. Whatever you do, don't carry any refreshments onto the approach. It takes just one spill to create a mess.

When another bowler is preparing to roll, don't talk to him. You may feel like ribbing a teammate or an opponent or you may want to crack a joke, but the time for that is *not* when someone is getting ready for a shot. Share your comments with others when both of you are off the lanes.

After you have stepped on the approach, wait until the pinsetting machine has completed its cycle of sweeping the pins off the lane and setting up those pins that should be there. If there is any mechanical problem with the machinery, notify the control desk.

Nearly every bowler becomes frustrated now and then with what he feels is bad luck. But no one appreciates a bowler who rants and raves, kicks the ball rack, stomps around or uses abusive language simply because the pins have not gone down. Such blowups are bothersome to everyone. So curb your temper. Besides, if you lose your cool you may become so upset that your game will fall apart.

Make an all-out effort not to loft the ball. Shots that sail more than two or three feet before landing on the lane will damage the playing surface, and that, in turn, will cause other problems. Damaged lanes require costly repairs and make it more difficult for bowlers—including yourself—to get a true roll when shots travel across those marred areas. If you just can't seem to overcome excessive lofting, do everyone a favor by asking for advice about how to correct this flaw. Lofting is not difficult to correct. And once you have learned how to get the ball down onto the lane properly you will almost surely be rewarding yourself, for a smoother shot is almost bound to help raise your scores.

TRAFFIC RULES

Although there are no traffic signals on the lanes, bowling proceeds in an orderly fashion because bowlers take their turns almost as methodically as if they were obeying red, yellow and green lights. When a bowler ahead of you has finished a shot, it is time for you to step up on the approach. Before you do so, however, glance to both sides to see if anyone on the adjacent lanes is already preparing to roll. If so, come to a stop, as if you have seen a red light. Don't go to the ball rack for your ball yet because this might disturb a bowler who is trying to concentrate on a shot. If no one is ready to bowl on the lanes immediately to the left and right, step onto the approach and get set for your shot. Some bowlers become overly cautious at this point, refusing to roll if someone two lanes away is already on the approach. This merely wastes time. Bowlers two lanes away should not be bothered by your presence and you should not be bothered by them.

If all is clear on the left and right—it is as if the green light has gone on —it is time for you to go. From the moment you get into your stance until you roll the ball down the lane should not take more than 5 or, at the most, 10 seconds. If you take longer you will be holding up the action: Bowlers on either side of you must wait for you, and so must the bowler behind you. If you spend 20 seconds during stance and delivery, that is at least 10 seconds too long. And if you take an extra 10 seconds an average of 15 times a game that adds up to 150 seconds—2½ minutes. Over a three-game block of league bowling, that comes out to 7½ minutes. That might seem harmless. It is not. League matches are scheduled to start at precise times. If you have held up your team's finish by some 7 minutes and another bowler has done the same, that means that the squad behind you will be roughly 14 minutes late in starting. Those teams will be even later if there is a third or a fourth bowler who has taken too much time on the lanes. No one likes to be delayed, so do your best to speed up your game if you find that you are a dawdler. If you are not guilty of this but someone else is, it would be wise for you or the team captain to talk to the straggler about the matter. Saving time will also save on people's nerves.

WARNING: STAY OUT. Such a sign would seem appropriate in some cases. A few bowlers, after completing their delivery, wander over onto the next lane as they try to coax their shots with lots of body English. This is a no-no. There is no penalty for such drifting, but it is obvious that it will interfere with other bowlers.

　　　　All these rules are simple enough. So is good sportsmanship. By congratulating an opponent who has made a nice shot or who has defeated you and by graciously accepting similar words from others, you will go a long way toward building friendly relations and making the game more enjoyable for all.

Glossary

ABC: American Bowling Congress, the world's largest sports-participation organization and the official rule-making body for tenpins.

AJBC: American Junior Bowling Congress.

Alley: The playing surface on which the ball is rolled and where the pins are located. Also known as a lane. In its plural form, can mean a bowling center.

Anchor: Last bowler in a team's lineup.

Angle: Direction of delivery; usually used to describe the shooting of spares when the ball goes across most of the lane. Also the path taken by a hook shot when it enters the strike pocket.

Approach: The area behind the foul line. Known, too, as the runway. Also the entire delivery process, from pushaway to release.

Arrows: Aiming aids embedded in the lane to help a bowler in targeting.

Baby Split: The 2-7 or 3-10 spare leaves.

Backup: A reverse hook. A shot that fades to the right for right-handers, to the left for left-handers.

Ball Rack: Where the ball rests before and after all shots. Also equipment to store house balls.

Bed: A lane or alley.

Bedposts: The 7-10 split.

Big Four: The 4-6-7-10 split. Also "big ears" and "double pinochle."

Blind: Score given to a team when a member is absent. Although based on the missing player's past performances, the score given is usually lower than the average for that bowler, thus penalizing him for the absence.

Block: An oil or lane-dressing buildup in the center of the lane, sometimes placed there illegally to help guide the ball to the strike zone and raise scores.

Blow: A missed spare.

Blowing a Rack: A resounding strike.

Boards: The strips of wood that make up a lane.

Box: A frame on the scoresheet. Ten of them constitute a game.

BPAA: Bowling Proprietors' Association of America.

Bridge: Distance between the finger holes on a ball.

Brooklyn: The 1-3 pocket for a left-hander, the 1-2 for a right-hander, both of which are "wrong-side" shots. Also, a cross, crossover, or "the Jersey side."

Bucket: The 2-4-5-8 or 3-5-6-9 leaves after the first ball is rolled.

Center: A bowling establishment.

Channel: The deeply grooved area on both sides of the lane. Also called the gutter.

Cherry: To chop or miss one of the back pins when the ball takes out only the front pin on a spare or a leave.

Christmas Tree: For left-handers, the 2-7-10 leave; for right-handers, the 3-7-10. Also, "Faith, Hope, and Charity."

Cincinnati: The 8-10 split.

Clean Game: To strike or spare in all 10 frames.

Clothesline: Either the 1-2-4-7 or the 1-3-6-10 leave.

Conditioning: Oiling or using lane dressing to prepare the lanes for play.

Cranker: A bowler who throws a ball that has a big hook at the end of its roll.

Crossover: A ball that crosses to the left of the headpin for right-handers, to the right of the headpin for left-handers.

Curve: A shot that moves in a wide-sweeping arc.

Deflection: The altered path of the ball after it hits a pin.

Double: Two consecutive strikes.

Drives: Archaic name for lanes.

Dutch 200: Rolling a 200 score by alternately making strikes and spares.

Error: Failing to convert a spare.

Fenceposts: The 1-2-4-7 or the 1-3-6-10 spare leaves.

Fill: The number of pins knocked down by the first ball after a spare. So called because those pins finish the scoring for the previous frame.

Foul: Touching or going beyond the foul line during delivery.

Foul Line: The dark line that separates the end of the approach from the head of the lane.

Foundation: A strike in the ninth frame.

Fudge Ball: A weak shot.

Grandma's Teeth: The 4-7-9-10 leave.

Graveyards: Lanes that are difficult to score on; an entire establishment known for low scores. Also called brickyards.

Greek Church: A split with three "steeples": the 6-9-10 on one side and two "steeples" on the other, the 4 and 7 pins.

Gutters: The deep grooves on either side of the lane.

Gutterball: A shot that rolls off the lane and into the gutter.

Handicap: Pins added to a bowler's score to equalize competition. The lower a bowler's average, the higher the handicap so that he or she will have a better opportunity to defeat a bowler with a higher average.

Heads: The first 16 feet of the lane beyond the foul line.

Headpin: The No. 1 pin; the "kingpin."

High Hit: A ball that enters the strike pocket more squarely on the head of the No. 1 pin than is desirable.

Hook: A ball that breaks sharply to the left for a right-hander, to the right for a left-hander.

Hooking Lane: One on which a ball hooks easily.

Holding Lane: One that tends to deter the hooking action of a ball.

Hole: The 1-2 pocket for lefties; the 1-3 pocket for righties.

House: A bowling center.

Inside: An angle, used primarily by professionals or high-average bowlers, in which the ball is started from the left of center by a right-hander, from the right of center by a left-hander.

Jersey Side: Same as "Brooklyn."

Kickbacks: Side partitions between the lanes at the pit end.

Lane: The playing surface. Also an alley.

Lane Dressing: A substance used to coat or condition the lane surface.

Leadoff: First bowler in a team's lineup.

Leave: Pins left standing after the first shot of a frame.

Lift: The upward motion applied to the ball by the fingers at the point of release.

Light Hit: A ball that enters the strike pocket by just barely nipping the No. 1 pin. Also a "thin hit."

Lily: The 5-7-10 split. Sometimes called the "Three Stooges" or "Hart, Schaffner & Marx."

Line: Path of a ball down the lane. Also a full game.

Lofting: Throwing the ball well out on the lane instead of rolling it smoothly.

Maples: Pins.

Mark: A strike or a spare.

Match Play: Two bowlers competing against one another.

Mixer: A shot that hits the pins at enough of an angle and with sufficient revolutions to cause a chain reaction in which many of them strike each other.

Mother-in-law: The 7 pin.

Murphy: The 2-7 or 3-10 splits.

NBC: National Bowling Council.

Nose Dive: Hitting the headpin flush in the midsection.

Nose Splits: Those resulting from hitting the headpin too flush.

Open: A frame without a strike or a spare.

Outside: The extreme right or left side of the lane. Used for describing shots that start out near the edge of the lane.

PBA: Professional Bowlers Association.

Perfect Game: A 300 score.

Pilgrim Ball: A weak shot; an "early settler."

Pit: The area below the far end of the lane into which the pins fall.

Pitch: The angle of the holes drilled in a ball.

Pocket: Between the 1 and 2 pins for left-handers; between the 1 and 3 pins for right-handers. The ideal place for the ball to hit the pins in an effort to obtain a strike.

Poison Ivy: The 3-6-10 leave.

Pointing: Aiming the ball.

Pot Game: A contest in which bowlers ante up an agreed-upon sum, which is then awarded to the high scorer or scorers.

Pumpkin: A weakly thrown ball.

Punch Out: To end a game by getting strikes on the last three or more shots.

Pushaway: Moving the ball into motion during the first step of the delivery.

Railroad: A split.

Rap: A pin that remains standing on what seemed to be a perfect shot.

Reading Lanes: Determining the subtle variations of lanes: where a track is, where dry and oily spots are, finding how much or how little a lane affects various types of shots.

Reverse Hook: A backup shot.

Rolloff: A match between individuals or teams to break a tie or settle a championship.

Running Lane: One on which the ball hooks easily.

Runway: The area immediately behind the foul line. Also called the approach.

Sanctioned: Any bowling competition conducted in accordance with the rules set down by the ABC or the WIBC. Also centers that meet the specifications of those organizations.

Sandbagger: A bowler who deliberately keeps his or her scores down to obtain a higher handicap, which can then be exploited by adding those pins when the person rolls as well as possible.

Schleifer: A strike on which the pins fall slowly.

Scratch: A bowler's actual score. Nonhandicap bowling.

Shadow Balls: Practice shots taken when no pins are set up on the lane.

Sleeper: A pin hidden behind another on a leave, such as the 9 on the 3-9 leave.

Slots: Lanes where it is relatively easy to roll high scores.

Span: The distance between the thumb hole and the finger holes on a ball.

Spare: Downing all 10 pins with two shots in one frame. Designated on the scoresheet with a /.

Splasher: A strike in which all the pins fall quickly.

Splice: Lane area where the maple and pine boards are joined.

Split: A spare leave in which the headpin is down and the remaining pins have another pin down immediately ahead of or between them so that the gap is greater than the width of the ball.

Spot: Target on the lane at which a bowler aims.

Stiff Lane: One not conducive to throwing a hook ball.

Strike: Knocking down all 10 pins with the first shot of a frame. Indicated on the scoresheet with an X.

Strike Out: Finishing a game with three or more strikes.

String: A succession of strikes.

Tap: A pin that remains standing on what apparently was a perfect hit.

Thunder in the Building: A thumping sound caused by a ball that rolls over the finger holes. The shot itself is called a "holy roller."

Track: An almost invisible path to the pins worn into the lane by balls that have been rolled in the same area.

Turkey: Three consecutive strikes.

Wall Shot: One in which pins bounce off the sideboards and then back toward the lane to topple another pin or pins.

Washout: A ball that cuts behind the headpin and creates any of the following leaves: the 1-2-10, the 1-2-4-10, the 1-3-7 or the 1-3-6-7.

WIBC: Women's International Bowling Congress.

WPBA: Women's Professional Bowlers Association.

Working Ball: A shot that drives solidly into the pins and creates plenty of mixing action.

YBA: Youth Bowling Association.

PICTURE CREDITS